A Girl's On-Course Survival Guide to Golf

Tee to Green and In-Between

I am an amateur player who can help you play well and survive on the golf course. I did it, and so can you. Clip this little guide onto your bag, and let's go!

By Christina Ricci

THOMAS NELSON
Since 1798

NASHVILLE   DALLAS   MEXICO CITY   RIO DE JANEIRO   BEIJING

© 2007 by The Media Game, LLC

Published in Nashville, Tennessee by Thomas Nelson.
Thomas Nelson is a registered trademark of Thomas Nelson, Inc.

Thomas Nelson, Inc titles may be purchased in bulk for educational, business, fundraising, or sales promotional use. For information, please e-mail SpecialMarkets@ThomasNelson.com.

This book is intended to provide accurate information with regard to the subject matter covered. However, the author and publisher accept no responsibility for inaccuracies, misinterpretations, or omissions, and the author and publisher specifically disclaim any liability, injury, loss, or risk, which is incurred as a consequence, directly or indirectly, of the use and/or application of any of the content in this book. The use of various marks throughout the book are not sponsor-related, and none endorse or are affiliated in any way with the author or publisher.

Rules and Etiquette copy reprinted by permission:
"10 Rules Golfers Break Most (Without Even Knowing It)"
Golf For Women Magazine, September/October 2004, and
"52 Etiquette Tips Every Golfer Must Know"
Golf For Women Magazine, May/June 2004.

Photography by Mario Muñoz Studio, Florida.
Illustrations by Robyn Neild, UK.

Edited by Pam Jaccarino and Lori Jones.

ISBN 978-1-4016-0375-5

Library of Congress Control Number: 2007937628

Printed in The United States of America
08 09 10 11 12 TWP 8 7 6 5 4 3

Acknowledgments

First and foremost I thank my mother for inspiring me
to create this book. I hope it is an inspiration and useful
tool for women golfers around the world. I would also
like to thank PGA professionals Kevin Sprecher, Master
Instructor of the Jim McLean Golf Academy, FL; Ray
Boone of the Ray Boone Golf Academy, FL; and Marc
Spencer of the Atkinson Resort and Country Club, NH;
for reviewing my book. I would like to thank VISION54® /
Coaching for the future® Inc., AZ, Lynn Marriott, and Pia
Nilsson for teaching me that golf is much more than a
technical pursuit. I would like to thank Carolyn Spachner
and Kevin Sprecher for providing access to a wonderful
golf course, Weston Hills CC, FL; Mario Muñoz, pictured

here, for taking
such wonderful
photographs;
Richard, my mother's
perpetual fiancé, for
introducing me to
this wonderful world
of golf; and Harry,
my biggest fan,
for all his support.
Lastly, I would like
to extend a special
thanks to my agent, Farley Chase, for his enthusiastic
support and guidance, as well as Pamela Clements for
sharing my vision.

About the **Author**

Who the heck is Christina Ricci? Is she the talented actress from the movie *The Addams Family*? No. But she is in the top percentile of excellent golfers in the country. The millions of women who love the game will find in Christina and this book an outreach and enthusiasm that are sure to spread. She's written this book because she wanted to share her five-year learning experience in a way that will inspire other amateur women golfers all over the world.

Christina didn't hire a ghostwriter. She wanted to do everything herself, including concept, production, and design, to ensure she got a book that was perfect for her audience. She wanted to create a full-color, visual book in which every page is a full image with short, concise, and easy-to-follow steps that would be utilized on the golf course. How does she do this and not be a LPGA/PGA professional? Simple—take what you know and how you got there, including the knowledge gained from all the lessons from her LPGA/PGA pros, and share them. The fundamentals are not originals, but they are solid fundamentals every golfer needs to be a good golfer. The goal was to create a hip, fun book with serious instruction.

I thank my mother...

I thank my mother for inspiring me to create *A Girl's On-Course Survival Guide to Golf* and the companion Web site. My mother began her golfing journey late in life, as many often do, and as I did. Over the last two years, I have watched her struggle through simple things such as chips, alignment, and shoulder turns. Mom was smart. She found a great PGA pro and took lessons. Her improvement has been tremendous. But as we all know, you then find yourself on the course, working on what your pro suggests. Great. But what about that sidehill lie that you and your pro didn't work on yesterday?

5 Handicap in 5 Years

Even though I am a 5 handicap, there are still times when I struggle with all the things a beginner struggles with, such as distance, chipping the ball closer, getting lower scores, and overcoming the mental obstacles that prevent all of us from playing great golf. I used to cut out articles from *Golf Digest*® and put them in my bag. Articles such as how to hit out of a deep rough, or what to do with a fried egg in the bunker. I would rummage through my bag in search for those golf tips. Then, I'd pull out the crinkled golf page, only to find I was holding up everyone.

I have compiled 284 pages of tried-and-true golf techniques. These are solid fundamentals, ones that helped me get from a 30 down to a 5 handicap in five years. The instruction and information in this book are visual and quick to grasp, with short steps of key points so you can execute the shot. So clip this little book onto your bag and let's get going…

What this guide **is**, what it **is not**, *and* **how** to use it.

This guide is your on-course survival guide to use while off the golf course, too. It covers everything you need to enjoy the game of golf and to score better, whether you are a weekend player, a corporate executive, or an avid golfer.

How many times are you at home, reading a great golf instruction book or magazine, and think, *Wow, what a great tip. I will try this tomorrow*? Tomorrow comes and you're facing the shot that you read about and, *oops*, you think, *What was that tip again? Is the ball up in my stance or back?!* Confusion sets in, and that's that. The tip is lost and so is the shot. Good news, girls: these tips are in this guide and easily accessible on the course.

Key fundamentals are spread throughout the guide; just look for the **KEY POINT** icon. And just in case you're down to your last ball, there are four **BAD-SHOT FIXES** sections: ON THE TEE BOX, ON THE FAIRWAY, AROUND THE GREEN, and ON THE GREEN. Rules and Etiquette, integral parts of the game, are included in their own section. If all else fails or if play is slow, have a few laughs, found in the golf JOKES section.

THIS GUIDE IS NOT MEANT TO REPLACE YOUR PRO. I am a strong believer that if you want to improve, search out the best instructors for you. Also, this guide is written for right handers.

look for these helpful icons along the way

RULES

ETIQUETTE

MENTAL

DO THIS

DON'T DO THIS

ADVANCED

I encourage you to visit the online companion to this Guide at www.GolfSurvivalGuide.com. It includes **TEE TO GREEN**, an online membership. **Watch, Listen and Learn** with more than one hundred videos and audio/visual

ONLINE MEMBERSHIP
TEE TO GREEN
A Girl's Off-Course Survival Guide to Golf™

lessons, a girl's forum, cool stuff to buy, lessons with top pros, and much more—all to help your game while **off the course**. Don't miss it!

Contents

Get to what you need FAST. No need to hold up the game, right girls?!

Cont'd next page ☞

"When warming up on the
range, do not take out your
driver first . . . I BEG YOU!"

Contents

"You didn't order that fried egg?"

Contents

LET'S GET STARTED!

GRIP LEFT HAND

The shaft is placed in the base of your fingers for optimum hinge, clubhead control, and feel.

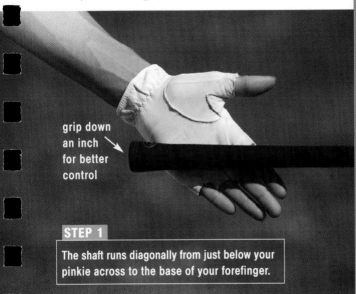

grip down
an inch
for better
control

STEP 1

The shaft runs diagonally from just below your pinkie across to the base of your forefinger.

DO grip down at least an inch from the butt of the shaft for more control.

DO THIS

STEP 2

Now just wrap your fingers excluding your thumb, around the shaft so it feels like the club is in your fingers.

GRIP LEFT HAND

heel of
your palm

STEP 3

Drop your thumb into place. When the left hand grip is complete, your thumb should sit just right of center, and the shaft should fit securely in the heel of your palm.

GRIP RIGHT HAND

The shaft is placed even more in your fingers
for optimum clubhead speed.

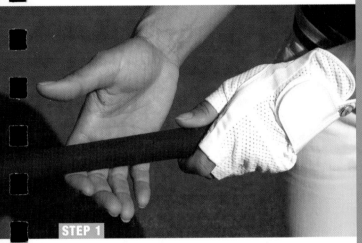

STEP 1

**The shaft runs diagonally from the base of your
pinkie across to the center of your index finger.**

STEP 2

**Close your right hand. Your
V should point to an area
between your right ear and
right shoulder.**

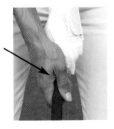

FINISHED
GRIP

YES

A Neutral Grip
Both V's created by your grip point to an area between your right ear and right shoulder, resulting in a square clubface at impact. Most common grip.

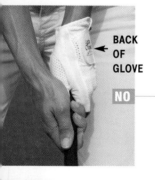

BACK OF GLOVE

NO

A Strong Grip
Both V's are pointing toward the outside of your right shoulder, and the back of your glove is almost entirely visible. This will cause a closed clubface at impact, which tends to make your ball go left. An anti-slice grip.

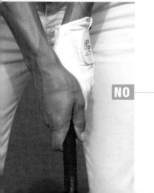

NO

A Weak Grip
Both V's are pointing toward your left shoulder. This will cause an open clubface at impact, which tends to make your ball go right. An anti-hook grip.

GRIP PRESSURE

is one of the most important aspects of your grip. Grip too tightly and you will not be able to hinge properly. Valuable clubhead speed and control will be lost. Grip too loosely and you will lose control of the club during mid-swing, accidently sending your club flying and knocking your buddy across the head.

STEP 1
Hold the club vertically, and notice how light the club and your grip feels.

STEP 2
Hold the club horizontally, and notice how heavy the clubhead feels.

STEP 3
Hold the club at a 45-degree angle. Your grip should feel firm enough to control the club, yet loose enough for proper hinge with relaxed arms and shoulders.

POSTURE

I see many women set up to the ball hunched over, their back and shoulders rounded and their chin pinned to their chest. You cannot swing freely in this setup.

YES

You can see that there is good space between my chest and chin, allowing room for my left shoulder to rotate freely on the backswing.

The shaft to spine visualization is a good method to use to feel consistent posture and to maintain that posture through the swing. As you turn into the backswing and come down through impact, visualize turning around the shaft without changing the shaft's angle. This will help you feel the correct spine angle and stay in your posture.

DOES YOUR CHEST GET IN THE WAY OF HITTING THE BALL?
THERE IS A SOLUTION.

Just because you are well-endowed doesn't mean you cannot hit a golf ball like your smaller-chested peers. There is a simple solution for large-chested women. At address, don't stand too upright; instead round off your shoulders. This allows your arms to hang away from your body, allowing more room to swing freely around those puppies.

POSTURE
FLEX-IT GIRL!

YES

POSTURE FOR POWER

A slight flex in your knees creates an athletic feel. A straight spine allows for your arms to hang down naturally. I feel centered, balanced, and ready to rip it.

NO
TOO RIGID, GIRL!

If you lock your knees, you take your legs out of the shot. To make matters worse, your posture will fluctuate in the backswing and downswing, resulting in power failure. You need your legs!

NO
If you flex too much, you will likely be too close to the ball, your arms will not hang freely, and your ball will not go very far.

YES

JUST RIGHT WITH MY DRIVER!
I am slightly wider than shoulder-width for good balance. For your mid-irons, your stance should be slightly narrower, and with your shorter irons even narrower.

STANCE
WITH YOUR DRIVER

A solid foundation is key to a balanced and powerful swing off the tee. If you are too narrow, balance will be jeopardized. If you are too wide, you will restrict your movement throughout your swing. If power is what you want, then a proper foundation is key, right, girls?

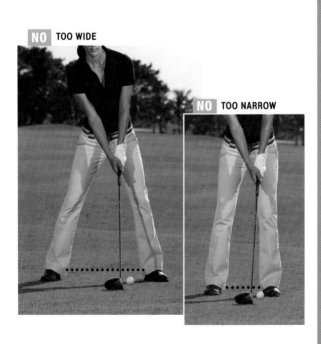

NO TOO WIDE

NO TOO NARROW

HAND POSITION
WITH A DRIVER

YES

With your driver, your hands should be about an inch behind the ball, with the shaft in line with your hands. This promotes an upward strike.

NO

NO

With your hands ahead of the ball, you will deliver a descending blow that results in a lower trajectory or pop-up.

ABOVE INSET PHOTO

For a mid-iron, your hands should be in line with the ball. With shorter clubs, it is OK to have your hands slightly ahead but not more than beyond your pants/skirt pocket.

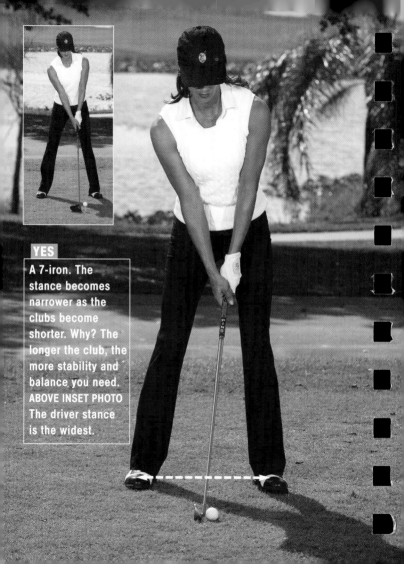

YES

A 7-iron. The stance becomes narrower as the clubs become shorter. Why? The longer the club, the more stability and balance you need. **ABOVE INSET PHOTO** The driver stance is the widest.

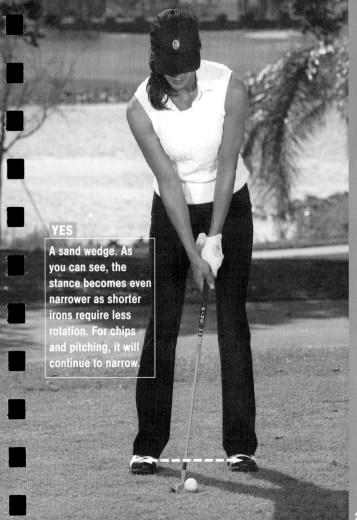

YES

A sand wedge. As you can see, the stance becomes even narrower as shorter irons require less rotation. For chips and pitching, it will continue to narrow.

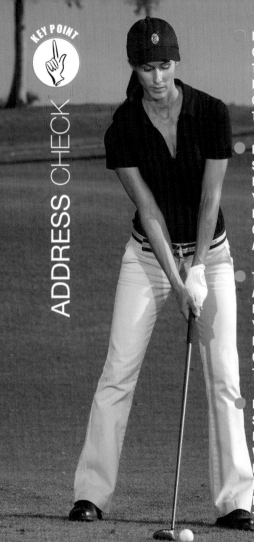

KEY POINT

ADDRESS CHECK

HEAD IS CLEAR OF NEGATIVE THOUGHTS, FOCUSED ONLY ON THE TARGET

RIGHT SHOULDER LOWER THAN YOUR LEFT, A RESULT OF GOOD POSTURE AND GRIP

TENSION-FREE, ARMS ARE RELAXED AND YOU ARE NOT DEATH-GRIPPING THE CLUB

BOTH KNEES SLIGHTLY FLEXED WITH YOUR RIGHT KNEE POINTING IN TOWARD TARGET

BALANCE CHECK

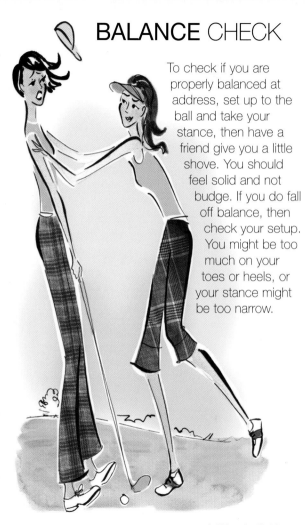

To check if you are properly balanced at address, set up to the ball and take your stance, then have a friend give you a little shove. You should feel solid and not budge. If you do fall off balance, then check your setup. You might be too much on your toes or heels, or your stance might be too narrow.

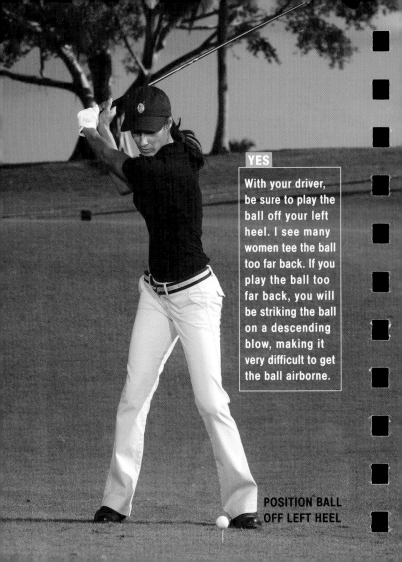

YES

With your driver, be sure to play the ball off your left heel. I see many women tee the ball too far back. If you play the ball too far back, you will be striking the ball on a descending blow, making it very difficult to get the ball airborne.

POSITION BALL OFF LEFT HEEL

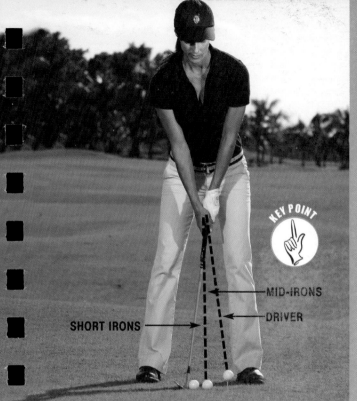

KEY POINT

MID-IRONS

DRIVER

SHORT IRONS

BALL POSITION

Improper ball position will lead your ball astray.
If your ball position is not correct, your club will
bottom out in the wrong spot, or you will
compensate with your body to adjust, which
you don't want to do.

ALIGNMENT

When determining your target and landing, always pick a specific target. This may sound like a simple task, but I see very few players do it.

Pick a specific target, as shown here. The second palm tree from the left is my target.

DO THIS

Pick an intermediate target. It makes the aim and alignment process much easier. Select a specific target. The more specific, the easier it is for your brain to register and get the ball to the intended target.

INCORRECT ALIGNMENT

Many players step into the ball with their body first. This is a backward approach. The result will most likely send the ball DEAD RIGHT for another bogey or double bogey.

NO

Many players address the ball with no awareness of the relationship between the ball, their body, and the target.

DITCH THE **HIP CHECK**

I see more players than I should attempt to align themselves to their target by placing a club on their hips. This is by no means accurate, ever! SO DITCH THE HIP CHECK, GIRLS!

STEP 1

Pick your target. In this photo, the target is the flag. Step into the shot behind the ball with your right foot. Aim the clubface to your intermediate target.

KEY POINT

CORRECT **ALIGNMENT**

The key to aligning yourself properly is to AIM THE CLUBFACE FIRST, with your body behind the ball looking toward your target.

STEP 2

Now set your feet, hips, and shoulders parallel to the target line.

Step into the shot with your right foot, aim the clubface, THEN set yourself.

Targets triceps and shoulders

Targets side

Targets quadracep

Targets upper and lower back

Targets calf

STRETCH
IT TAKES JUST TEN MINUTES

Warming up your muscles before and during a round helps eliminate those stiffed-leg, no-turn shots to the right.

Targets hamstring

76

STRETCH BEFORE AND

Targets lower forearm

Targets pectoral and bicep

DURING YOUR ROUND

Targets upper forearm

RANGE PLAY

When warming up for a round, start with your sand wedge and work your way up to your driver. The goal on the range is to get your tempo for the day and to loosen up those stiff muscles.

YES

Lay a club perpendicular to the target line for precise ball position. Then lay a club left and parallel to the target line for proper alignment.

DON'T DO THIS

Don't just hit twenty
driver shots as hard
and fast as you can,
and then head to the
tee with that tempo.
You can be certain
you will hit a few in
the woods. Instead,
when warming up
on the range, pick
different targets,
clubs, and yardages.

CHIP AND PUTT

YES

Warm up with a variety of shots around the green. Pick shots you think you will need on the course. Good ones are chips from the fringe, high soft shots from the rough, low runners, and sand shots.

Chips just off the green are always good to practice. You can get the feel of the greens and how the ball rolls that day.

Again, the purpose of warming up around the green before a round is to find your feel and tempo for the day. Every day is different, so don't expect the same feel as last time.

YES
Practice high soft shots from the rough.

YES

PRACTICE YOUR UP-AND-DOWNS. Why? The goal of practice is to simulate course conditions so you can score better out on the course. Putting five balls in a row from the same spot is fine if you are working on your putting technique. However, do practice your up-and-downs to improve your scoring ability. Chip to a hole and then putt. Change the shot each time. This kind of practice gives you confidence to get up-and-down on the course.

PRE-SHOT
ROUTINE
A GOOD ONE
TO FOLLOW

①

**FROM BEHIND
THE BALL**
pick your
primary and
intermediate
target.

MENTAL

Many players get to the tee box, pick the center of the fairway, set up to the ball, AND THINK AND THINK AND THINK about everything including that nice pair of shoes at Neiman's. Fear, indecision, and tension are the ingredients in this routine. Not a good recipe for a solid shot. Instead, you want TOTAL COMMITMENT TO THE SHOT.

Make your intentions very clear and very positive.

Instead, make all of your decisions behind the ball while looking out to the target. Notice the wind direction, pick a primary target and an intermediate target, and envision your line of flight. Make your intentions clear. Now set up to the ball, feel the shot, see the target, and go. This is a successful recipe that will give you much more consistency.

Develop a ROUTINE you can TRUST:

- It keeps you calm.
- It keeps you in the present.
- It keeps you consistent.
- It keeps your energy focused on one thing: executing this shot—not the next shot or the last shot, THIS SHOT.

② **VISUALIZE YOUR SHOT** Take a couple of easy swings while checking the wind and visualizing the line of flight.

③

AIM YOUR CLUBFACE
Confident with your plan, step into the shot with your right foot, aim the clubface to your intermediate target.

Then set yourself by making sure your feet, hips, and shoulders are parallel and left of the target.

④

RIP IT!
Take a final look at your target, waggle, and rip it.

HOW TO TEE IT UP

So many tees, so little time! There are so many tees on the market today that it can get confusing. Most tees are conventional height, but with today's gigantic drivers, there are tees that are four inches high! Follow the tried-and-true methods below to avoid tee confusion.

YES DRIVER: TEE IT UP ½ INCH ABOVE TOP OF DRIVER

½ inch high from top of driver

ADVANCED

DRIVER TEE OPTIONS
IF YOU WANT TO GET FANCY TRY
THESE TEE HEIGHTS

To promote a draw, tee the ball up higher. Just remember, your angle of attack should have a more in-to-out path with a flatter swing plane. To promote a fade, tee the ball lower. Just remember, your downswing plane should have a slightly steeper angle of attack, which encourages a left-to-right ball flight.

YES LONG IRONS: 1/2 INCH HIGH FROM THE GROUND

just above grass
for shorter irons

WHERE TO TEE IT UP

Most players head straight for the middle of the tee box to tee their ball. Instead, use the entire tee box to your advantage. A good rule of thumb is to tee it up on the side of trouble. Visually, it is a better angle to aim away from the trouble and into the fairway.

ADVANCED

If you want to draw the ball, tee it up on the left side of the tee box and draw the ball back to the center. For a fade, tee it up on the right side and shape the shot back to the center of the fairway.

I WANT MORE DISTANCE AND I WANT IT NOW!!!

RHYTHM AND TEMPO

I cannot stress enough the importance of RHYTHM and TEMPO. Without them, errant shots will be the norm and consistency will be a difficult suitor.

You want to take control of the club, not the club taking control of you, right, girls?! Know when you are swinging out of your socks, then STOP IT! Take three deep breaths and, literally, cut your swing tempo in half.

MENTAL

A FACT: When your swing goes awry, you tend to quicken your tempo. The more it goes awry, the faster the tempo gets. Why? Confidence is lost and self-doubt creeps in, resulting in a desperate attempt to make contact. TRY THIS: The next time you feel your tempo skyrocketing, COMMIT TO SWINGING AT 50 PERCENT ON EVERY SWING—in both backswing and downswing. After several swings, you will begin to feel your natural tempo return. It works, trust me!

THE TAKE-AWAY
MAINTAIN THE TRIANGLE

YES

MAINTAIN THE TRIANGLE
As you begin your backswing, think about maintaining the triangle by keeping your hands, arms, and shoulders moving together in one piece. It keeps the club on the right path and promotes a wide arc—the key for more distance.

HALFWAY BACK
At this point in the backswing your club should be parallel to the target line.

NO

TOO INSIDE
As you begin your backswing, AVOID pulling the club too inside. If you pull inside, you will most likely snap hook or push the shot to the right to compensate for your clubhead being too far behind your hands.

KEY POINT

BACKSWING
TAKE-AWAY KEYS

- At the start of your backswing, maintain the triangle formed at address.

- Smooth, even tempo is key. Avoid quick, jerky movements.

- Shaft should be parallel to target line halfway back.

BACKSWING
The L-shaped right elbow is
better than the "flying right elbow"

YES

JUST RIGHT
Notice how the
right elbow points
down and creates
an L shape. The
result of a good
take-away and turn.
This promotes a
wide arc, which is
key to **MORE
DISTANCE.**

NO

THE FLYING ELBOW
The space between the right side and elbow is too great. A "flying elbow" is typically the result of a fast and disconnected take-away. You will not get good DISTANCE with this elbow action.

NO

THE SHORT "V"
The space between the right side and elbow is too little, resulting in a V. This narrows your arc, restricts your movement, and adds NO DISTANCE.

STRETCH EQUALS POWER

90°

45°

YES

A GOOD RATIO
40- to 50-degree
hip turn and 90- to
95-degree shoulder
turn equals POWER
AND DISTANCE.

IF YOU WANT POWER, then you need a GOOD STRETCH. Think of a rubber band. When you pull it back, you can feel the torque. When you release the rubber band, it jumps off your fingers. Same deal with the backswing. You need to CREATE RESISTANCE in relation to your hip and your shoulder turn. Most players have too much hip turn, zapping the rubber band effect and thus zapping power and distance.

100°

65°

NO

NO TORQUE
65-degree hip turn
and 90 to 100-degree
shoulder turn, equals
LESS POWER AND
DISTANCE.

YES

SQUARE CLUBFACE AT THE TOP
OF YOUR BACKSWING means
less work on the downswing.
Ideally, the clubface should be
parallel with your left forearm.

Do make a big
shoulder turn
so that your
left shoulder
sits under
your chin—a
sign of a good
turn for lots of
POWER.

DO THIS

KEY POINTS FOR A SOLID BACKSWING

- **FULL SHOULDER TURN, YOUR BACK IS FACING THE TARGET**

- **LEFT ARM STRAIGHT, TO PROMOTE A WIDE ARC, NOT BENT OR TOO RIGID**

- **SHOULDERS TURNED MORE THAN HIPS TO CREATE TORQUE**

- **RIGHT KNEE STILL FLEXED AT TOP OF THE BACKSWING**

- **RIGHT TOE SLIGHTLY OPEN TO PROMOTE AN UNRESTRICTED TURN**

KEY POINT

KEY POINTS FOR
A SOLID DOWNSWING

- **YOUR HEAD IS
  QUIET AND
  BEHIND THE BALL**

- **LEFT SHOULDER
  HIGHER THAN RIGHT,
  A GOOD INDICATION YOU
  ARE STAYING IN YOUR
  POSTURE**

- **CLUBFACE SQUARE
  AT IMPACT AND HANDS
  SLIGHTLY AHEAD, A GOOD
  INDICATION YOU HAVE
  NOT UNHINGED YOUR
  WRISTS TOO EARLY**

- **GOOD WEIGHT
  SHIFT ONTO
  LEFT SIDE,
  RIGHT FOOT
  ALMOST ON TOE**

PLANE AND SIMPLE

To optimize your chances of hitting solid shots, you need to be on plane. This means as you begin your downswing, the butt of the shaft is pointing at or just near the ball. If the shaft is above the ideal plane line, you will most likely come over the top as the plane would be too steep. If it is below (too flat), you would most likely flip your hands through impact, resulting in a duck hook or conversely, a blocked shot to the right.

above the plane

under the plane

← ― finish is
   upright
   and
   forward

YES

A GOOD
FINISH IS ONE
IN WHICH
90 PERCENT
OF YOUR
WEIGHT is on
your front foot.
A sign of a
swing with
good tempo.

nice weight
transfer

FINISH IN BALANCE

An under-rated topic. Most players finish with fancy footwork—completely off-balance. You should be able to watch the ball hit the ground in perfect balance on your finish. Why so important? Without a balanced finish, in which 90 percent of your weight is on your front foot, you will suffer back pain, inconsistency in shot making, and too many swear words under your breath!

OUCH!! A REVERSE C

NO
A BAD FINISH.
This is a sure way to send your ball off-line and cause some serious back pain.

too much weight on my back foot

① OFF PLANE

YES

GOOD POSITION!
This means the shaft is parallel to your target. From here, the club can **DROP IN THE "SLOT" ON THE DOWNSWING.**

BAD-SHOT FIXES

MAIN CAUSES OF
SLICES AND HOOKS

① **OFF PLANE** Backswing and/or downswing

② **POOR ALIGNMENT** Misalignment results in compensations in the downswing to get the clubface back to square at impact.

③ **FAST TEMPO AND TENSION** throws off your swing's sequence.

NO

ACROSS THE LINE
This means the shaft is pointing to the right of your target. From here your downswing plane will most likely be too inside, thus causing a **HOOK OR PUSH TO THE RIGHT.**

NO

LAID-OFF CLUB
This means the shaft is pointing to the left of your target. From here, you will most likely take an out-to-in path, causing a **SLICE OR PULL TO THE LEFT.**

② POOR ALIGNMENT
an open stance and what it does

NO

AN OPEN STANCE
This means you are aiming too far left with your feet, hips, and shoulders in relation to the target line.

NO

AN OPEN STANCE might result in an open CLUBFACE AT IMPACT. This means because you set up too OPEN at address, you will most likely not release in time and you will BLOCK YOUR SHOT TO THE RIGHT, or YOU MIGHT FLIP YOUR HANDS in an effort to square the clubface.

YES

GOOD DOWNSWING! Notice how the backswing and downswing almost mirror each other. Your downswing should follow a path that is slightly under the backswing plane.

75

② POOR ALIGNMENT
a closed stance and what it does

NO

A CLOSED STANCE
This means you are aiming too far RIGHT with your feet, hips, and shoulders in relation to the target line.

NO

DUCK HOOK
This means because you set up too **CLOSED** at address, you will most likely come across your body, causing a **LOW BIG HOOK, A.K.A. DUCK HOOK.**

POOR ALIGNMENT = POOR RESULTS

NO

OVER THE TOP
Because you are set up too **CLOSED** at address, you will most likely swing from too **OUTSIDE AND TOO VERTICAL** a path on the downswing, causing a **LEFT-TO-RIGHT BALL FLIGHT** or "SLICE."

③ FAST TEMPO AND TENSION

throws off your swing's natural sequence, making it very difficult to square the face

NO

FAST TEMPO ON THE DOWNSWING
Your hips outrace your hands. From here it will be difficult to square the clubface.

TAI-CHI SWING

While attending a GOLF54® three-day golf school in Arizona, I learned about the Tai-Chi swing. I was asked to take my stance and make a full swing but at the slowest speed possible. Literally, a three-minute swing. What this does is show you where you are at each point in your swing and gives you more awareness of where you need to be.

NO

NO CONTROL OF YOUR CLUB IN THE BACKSWING. It is very difficult to control the club if your tempo is fast. A fast backswing can result in a reverse pivot or overswinging.

A SLOWER BACKSWING allows you to feel the top of your backswing so you can make a **SMOOTH TRANSITION** into the downswing.

MENTAL

ON THE TEE BOX BAD-SHOT FIXES

BAD-SHOT FIXES
MAIN CAUSES OF
NO DISTANCE

① **UNSTABLE BASE** The lateral slide can result in power failure.

② **WRIST HINGE** Lack of wrist hinge can cause power leaks.

③ **BACKSWING NO-NO'S:**
OVERSWINGING A false sense of power.
FAKE TURN Turn, don't lift!

① UNSTABLE BASE
the lateral slide = power failure

A DISTANCE KILLER

I cannot stress enough the importance of
A SOLID BASE. This is your power source.
Your distance comes from a solid, braced right
leg. If you slide, you lose all YOUR POWER.

Cont'd next page ☞

NO

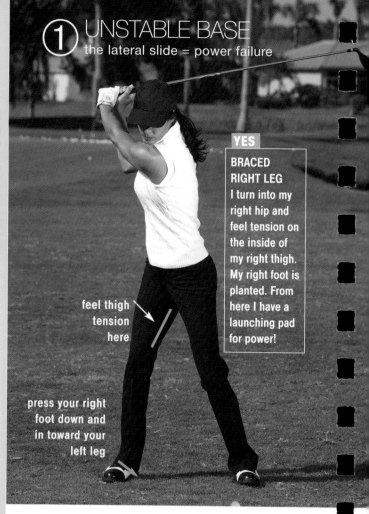

① UNSTABLE BASE
the lateral slide = power failure

YES

BRACED RIGHT LEG
I turn into my right hip and feel tension on the inside of my right thigh. My right foot is planted. From here I have a launching pad for power!

feel thigh tension here

press your right foot down and in toward your left leg

slide - bad

NO

THE SLIDE—THE SWAY
Notice my right knee has collapsed, also causing my right foot to come off the ground. From this position, my weight will not transfer properly to the left side. From here, I will most likely throw the club from the top instead of using the leverage from a braced right leg to initiate the downswing.

② WRIST HINGE
lack of wrist hinge = power leaks

Not enough hinge

NO

NO HINGE MEANS NO DISTANCE
The angles in my wrists are minimal. You need wrist hinge; otherwise, you will have nothing to release through the impact zone!

YES Good hinge

DO THIS

As you address the ball, grip the club lightly and waggle your wrists, making sure they remain loose. If you are death-gripping the club there will be no wrist hinge.

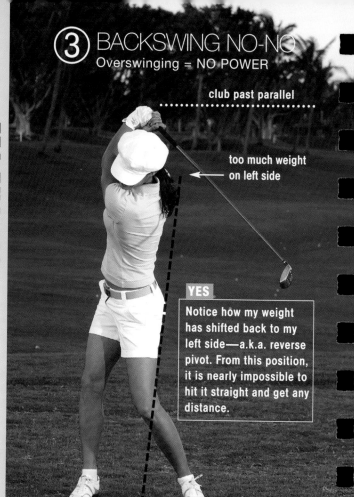

③ BACKSWING NO-NO
Overswinging = NO POWER

club past parallel
....

too much weight
on left side

YES

Notice how my weight
has shifted back to my
left side—a.k.a. reverse
pivot. From this position,
it is nearly impossible to
hit it straight and get any
distance.

YES

Weight shift is good here. You can see that 80 percent of weight has shifted to my right side. From here I can explode into the downswing.

DO THIS

KEEP YOUR KNEES WIDE to prevent overswinging and promote a solid base to turn. Visualize a ball between your knees on the backswing.

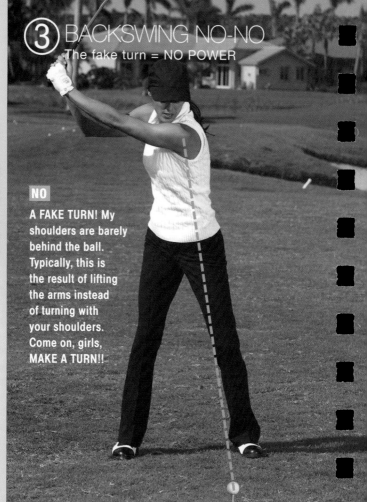

3 BACKSWING NO-NO
The fake turn = NO POWER

NO

A FAKE TURN! My shoulders are barely behind the ball. Typically, this is the result of lifting the arms instead of turning with your shoulders. Come on, girls, MAKE A TURN!!

YES

A BIG TURN means your shoulders are behind the ball and your back is facing the target.

SWING SEQUENCE

YES

Good rule of thumb for shorter irons: play the ball in the center of your stance (shown here).

1-2 inches left of center for longer irons

CONSISTENT IRONS

Ball position plays an important roll in solid contact. With longer irons, if you play the ball too far back (right of center), you will not have enough time to release the club. If you play the ball too far forward, you will need to lunge at the ball to get to it in time.

hit down

IRON PLAY
HIT DOWN ON THE BALL

Many women players are afraid to hit down on the ball (I was one of them). They fear they will chunk the ball and hurt themselves, so they try to lift or "scoop" the ball off the turf. If you do not hit down on the ball, you will not achieve airtime, distance, and backspin, the three components of a solid shot.

If you want this ball to get airborne, then hit down, girls!

TENSION IN THE ARMS AND SHOULDERS will make it difficult to hit down and through (release). It took me a long time to understand this concept. With tense arms, I used to hold on for dear life and top the ball every

MENTAL

time. Now with relaxed arms, I am able to extend down and through. If this is your tendency, try this: Test your grip pressure by **THROWING A CLUB** (literally) to your target. If the club ends up way left of your target or behind you, you are holding on for dear life. Your goal is to get the club to your target.

YES

GOOD POSITION! Ball position is about 2-3 inches ahead of center and the shaft is vertical, meaning the butt of the club is not pushed forward or back.

WOODS IN THE FAIRWAY
NOT IN THE WOODS

I see many women top their woods in an effort to help the ball in the air or, conversely, their angle of attack is steep in an effort to hit down on the ball. Woods are intended to sweep the ball off the grass with little or no divot. Their wider sole and bigger head are more forgiving, thus easier to hit than irons. I like to think low, slow, and wide on the take-away, which helps me maintain a nice sweeping action for a ball that goes a mile.

set your wrists early

DO THIS

Do set your wrists early, as shown here, for optimum distance.

KNOW YOUR DIVOTS

YES

A GOOD DIVOT
A sign that the clubhead contacted the ball on the correct plane—not too deep and not too shallow, which would produce no divot at all.

Learn from your divots—they can tell you what you may be doing incorrectly in your swing.

NO

A BAD DIVOT—TOO BIG AND WRONG ANGLE. If your divot looks like this, you are most likely slicing the ball by coming over-the-top. This divot is also too deep—a sign that the downswing angle was too steep.

YES

PERFECT FOR LIES LIKE THIS. I need height to get over these palm trees. My rescue club is the perfect club for the job.

HYBRIDS
THE RESCUE CLUB

Why is it called the rescue club? It is easier
to hit out of tall grass or funky lies with the
rescue club. The clubface is shallower, similar
to your woods. So the setup is the same. The
hybrids are your replacement for the long
irons in your bag such as the 3 and 4.

LIP →

YES

**PERFECT LIE
AND POSITION**
I have plenty of
room in this
bunker to clear
the lip.

7 WOOD
PERFECT IN A FAIRWAY BUNKER

If your lie allows in a fairway bunker, the 7-wood is the club to use. Why? It is an easier club to hit because you sweep the ball off the sand for a CLEAN HIT THAT GOES A MILE. Just make sure you are far enough from the lip of the bunker and make sure your ball is sitting pretty. If it is buried, use a short iron to punch the ball out.

In a fairway bunker, **DO STAND UP TALLER** to promote hitting the ball first. Do try your hybrid if you do not have a 7-wood.

KNOW YOUR DISTANCES

Miscalculating how far you hit a shot with each club costs strokes. My mother is a perfect example. I will ask her what club she is using for a shot that is 80 yards to the pin, with no wind. "An 8-iron," she says. Of course, the ball goes well over the green.

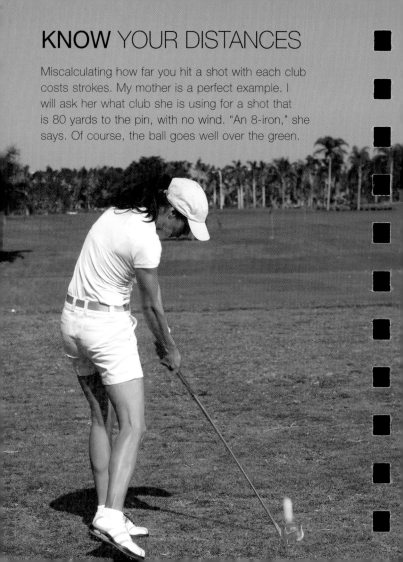

AVERAGE DISTANCES
15+ HANDICAPPER

WIND CONDITIONS →	NONE	BEHIND	FRONT
DRIVER	185	190	180
3 WOOD	165	170	160
4 IRON	155	160	150
5 IRON	145	150	140
6 IRON	135	140	130
7 IRON	125	130	120
8 IRON	115	120	110
9 IRON	105	110	100
PW	90	95	85
SW	60	65	55

CLUB SELECTION

Girls, I know many times, especially just starting out, you feel more confident with overclubbing. You will score much better and faster though, if you know how far you hit each club, and trust it.

① HEAD IS AHEAD

NO

HEAD RACES AHEAD
If your head initiates the downswing and gets ahead of the ball, you will top the ball. This means you will hit the top (SKULL) half of the ball sending it NOWHERE.

BAD-SHOT FIXES
MAIN CAUSES OF
THIN AND FAT

1. **HEAD IS AHEAD** If your head gets ahead of the ball through impact, FORGETABOUTIT.

2. **POOR IMPACT** Trying to scoop or flip the ball instead of hitting down on the ball.

3. **IMPROPER SEQUENCE** If your lower body outraces your upper body, FORGETABOUTIT.

YES

HEAD STAYS BEHIND so your hips and arms can pass freely AND the downswing stays on the correct inside-out path.

② POOR IMPACT
scoop or flip instead of hitting down

THIN AND FAT ON THE FAIRWAY

NO

A BIG NO-NO, the clubhead outraces the hands. This results in a left wrist breakdown, resulting in a scoop or flip of the hands AND MOST LIKELY A "CHUNKY MONKEY."

a scoop

YES

GREAT IMPACT!
Hands are still ahead
of the clubhead,
resulting in a
descending blow
and solid strike.

flat wrist

③ IMPROPER SEQUENCE

Don't get too fast with your hips on the downswing. This was my nemesis. The key is to drop your hands into the slot by slightly shifting your lower body to the left, MORE OF A WEIGHT TRANSFER THAN A SLIDE. Do not lunge your lower body left like you see here. Unless I flip my hands or use my body to square the club, THIS BALL IS GOING RIGHT AND THIN.

Notice how my hips have outraced my hands. From here, I have to exert extra energy to get the club on the ball. INSTEAD, my hands need to be more in front of my right hip pocket.

MAIN CAUSES OF

NO DISTANCE

① **NOT ENOUGH LAG** Unhinging your wrists
too early in the downswing

② **BACKSWING NO-NO'S** Overswinging, left arm
breakdown, hip slide on take-away

③ **CHICKEN WING RELEASE** Holding on for dear life

the hosel - - - - ➤

THE "S" WORD
THE DREADED SHANK

Definition: When your ball shoots violently to the right.
WHY? It results from hitting the ball off the hosel instead
of square in the middle of the clubface. To fix, make sure
you are not standing too close to the ball AND, on the
short shots, STAY WITH THE SHOT—NO PEEKING. I have
shanked when I lifted my head too early through the shot.

NO DISTANCE ON THE FAIRWAY

① NOT ENOUGH LAG

YES

GOOD ANGLES EQUAL POWER Shown here, my wrists are still hinged (cocked) which delivers the necessary speed for a solid strike. If you unhinge TOO early, you will release all the energy before it reaches the ball, resulting in LESS DISTANCE.

② BACKSWING NO-NO
OVERSWINGING

NO

OUCH! Club is way beyond parallel, weight is still on left side, and I am not turned behind the ball.

Weight never got transferred to the inside of my right heel, still here.

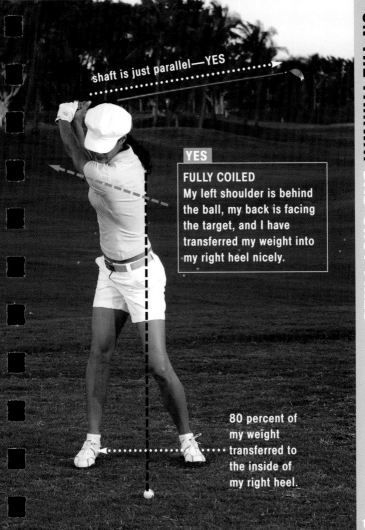

shaft is just parallel—YES

YES

FULLY COILED
My left shoulder is behind the ball, my back is facing the target, and I have transferred my weight into my right heel nicely.

80 percent of my weight transferred to the inside of my right heel.

② BACKSWING NO-NO
LEFT ARM BREAKDOWN

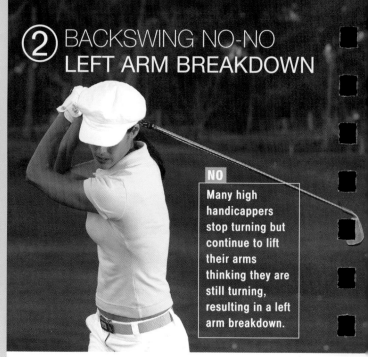

NO

Many high handicappers stop turning but continue to lift their arms thinking they are still turning, resulting in a left arm breakdown.

LEFT ARM POSITION
WIDER IS BETTER

YES

WIDE ARC PROMOTES POWER AND DISTANCE! The key to a wide arc is the SHOULDER TURN. As you turn, you want your hands as far from your head as possible. Feel your shoulders turn and your arms as an extension of your shoulders, working together, not independently.

The golf swing travels on an arc. A bigger arc equals more distance. If your left arm breaks down on the backswing, you are shortening the swing radius, thus killing any chance for good distance.

YES

Notice how my hips have turned and have not slid past the dotted line. Feel tension on the inside of your upper right thigh to avoid this deadly move.

Feel your right foot pressing down and in toward your left leg.

②

BACKSWING NO-NO
LATERAL SLIDE
HIP SLIDE ON THE TAKE-AWAY

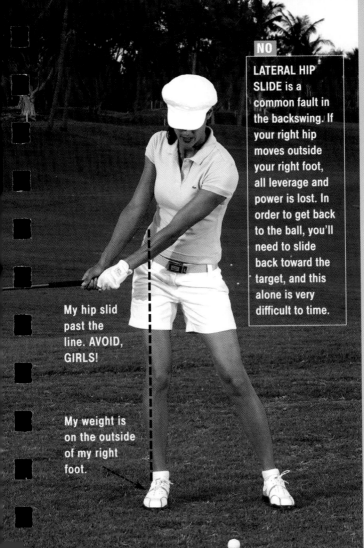

NO

LATERAL HIP SLIDE is a common fault in the backswing. If your right hip moves outside your right foot, all leverage and power is lost. In order to get back to the ball, you'll need to slide back toward the target, and this alone is very difficult to time.

My hip slid past the line. AVOID, GIRLS!

My weight is on the outside of my right foot.

YES

FULLY EXTENDED PAST IMPACT
My right forearm crossing over left forearm as a result of rotating my body left and letting my arms extend down toward the target line.

(3) CHICKEN WING
RELEASE

HOLDING ON FOR DEAR LIFE

DO THIS Consistent grip pressure from the start of your swing to the finish will lead to more consistent ball striking.

NO

If you hold on to the club through the impact zone, you will resemble this look. To avoid this dreaded look, make sure that you are not tensing-up through the impact zone. Tension in your shoulders, arms, or hands will lead your ball off-line.

YES

THE PROPHECY WILL COME TRUE. Always think about where you want the ball to go, NOT where you don't want the ball to go. The ball will go where your thoughts and energy go.

MENTAL

PLAYING IN THE SAND DIVOT

Yes, there are those shots that find these craters. No worries. Just think of this shot as a fairway bunker shot, except here you can ground your club.

STEP 1

PLAY THE BALL BACK IN YOUR STANCE
This will ensure you catch the ball first.

STEP 2

SWING DOWN AND THROUGH This will ensure that you do not try to scoop the ball off the sand or dig a hole to China!

intended
target

a right to left shot

SHAPING THE SHOT
HOW TO HIT A DRAW

It is all in your setup. Keep in mind, because of the right-to-left spin, the ball tends to go farther. It is a controlled hook.

STEP 1

Aim the clubface to your intended target.

STEP 2

Now CLOSE your stance, meaning aim your feet, hips, and shoulders RIGHT of your target line.

STEP 3

Tee the ball slightly HIGHER than you normally would (half the ball sits above the driver is normal), promoting a flatter, more in-to-out swing path.

STEP 4

Now make your normal swing. Because of your setup, the path of the club will be more in-to-out promoting a right-to-left ball flight.

a left to right shot

intended
target

SHAPING THE SHOT
HOW TO HIT A FADE

It is all in your setup. Keep in mind a fade tends to go higher and therefore has less roll. It is a controlled slice.

STEP 1

Aim the clubface to your intended target.

STEP 2

Now **OPEN** your stance, meaning aim your feet, hips, and shoulders **LEFT** of your target line.

STEP 3

Tee the ball slightly **LOWER** than you normally would, promoting a descending blow, which tends to put a left-to-right spin on the ball.

STEP 4

Now make your normal swing. Because of your setup, the path of the club will be more out-to-in, promoting a left-to-right ball flight.

SHAPING THE SHOT
HOW TO HIT A LOW HOOK

Again, like the draw off the tee, it is all in your setup.
You want to feel like you're sweeping the ball off the turf.

ball
finishes
here

ball starts
right of
palm tree

ADVANCED

Do maintain a light grip pressure to ensure that you release the clubface.

STEP 1

Play the ball back in your stance.

STEP 2

Aim your clubface to where you want THE BALL TO FINISH. In the photo, I want my ball to land in the fairway just left of the palm tree.

STEP 3

Aim your feet, hips, and shoulders where you want the BALL TO START. In the photo, the ball starts right of the palm tree.

STEP 4

Now make your normal swing. Because of your setup, the path of the club will have a slightly more in-to-out path, promoting a right-to-left ball flight.

SHAPING THE SHOT
HOW TO HIT A SHARP CUT

Again, like the fade, it is all in your setup.

ball starts
left of
palm tree

ball
finishes
here

A slightly tighter grip pressure will keep the clubface open to help create a cut.

STEP 1

Play the ball back in your stance for a lower trajectory, but farther ahead if you need more height.

STEP 2

Aim your clubface where you want THE BALL TO FINISH. In the photo, I want my ball to land in the fairway just right of the palm tree.

STEP 3

Aim your feet, hips, and shoulders where you want the BALL TO START.

STEP 4

Now make your normal swing. Because of your setup, the path of the club will have a slightly more out-to-in path, promoting a left-to-right ball flight.

OVER A TREE

Don't panic. There is an easy way to get over a tree. It starts with a setup very similar to a fade. One key factor in determining if you should attempt this is your lie. If half the ball or more is sitting on top of the grass, go for it. If only a quarter or less is visible don't even try it. Pitch it out with a pitching wedge.

STEP 1

Play the ball farther ahead in your stance as you need the height, and widen your stance just a bit.

STEP 2

Take dead aim at the tree and set your feet, hips, and shoulders slightly open to the target, so aim your body lines left of the target (the tree).

STEP 3

Take your normal swing. Because of your setup, your swing path will be steeper, which is necessary to get the ball airborne quickly.

THE KEY TO SUCCESS IS 100 PERCENT COMMITMENT. Visualize the ball sailing over the tree. Have NO DOUBT and you will succeed.

UNDER A TREE

There is an easy way to get under a tree's limbs. To achieve this, you will need to keep the ball low and control the three things that elevate a ball's flight: loft, clubhead speed, and backspin. So good news for you girls that don't like to hit down with your irons. This will feel more like a long, low chip shot.

STEP 1

Use a 3-, 4-, or 5-iron. Play the ball farther back in your stance. This will tilt the shaft forward and de-loft the club (take the loft out of the iron) so the ball flight will be low.

STEP 2

Make a three-quarter backswing at 50-percent speed. A slower speed reduces the backspin on the ball, which in turn reduces its chances of getting airborne.

STEP 3

On the downswing, you want to feel like you finish lower with your hands, almost like you are making a long chip shot. A lower finish helps keep the ball low.

STEP 1

ASSESS YOUR LIE.
Is the ball sitting up or
down in the grass? If
sitting down, just pitch it
out. If the ball is sitting up,
than take one less club
than you normally would.
The more grass between
the club and the ball the
hotter the ball will come
off the club, meaning the
ball will have less spin.

PLAY ROUGH
DON'T LET THE ROUGH, ROUGH YOU UP.

STEP 2

HOVER THE CLUB so it doesn't snag on your takeaway. Play the ball in the middle of your stance. Place more weight on your front foot. Grip down an inch or so and stand closer to the ball. This will promote a steeper backswing and a cleaner strike.

STEP 3

TAKE A DIVOT, and think steady acceleration. You do not want to jab at the ball. **STRIKE DOWN AND THROUGH.**

STEP 1

Set up to the ball
with an open stance
and open clubface.
My legs are quieter
in this swing, so I
like to take a wider
stance for more
stability.

FLOP SHOT

The flop shot is a last-resort shot. It should only be used, for example, if you need to get over a bunker and there is very little green (tight pin).

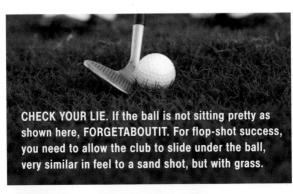

CHECK YOUR LIE. If the ball is not sitting pretty as shown here, FORGETABOUTIT. For flop-shot success, you need to allow the club to slide under the ball, very similar in feel to a sand shot, but with grass.

STEP 2

ACCELERATE ON THE DOWNSWING, sliding the club under the ball.

DO THIS

DO MAINTAIN a light grip pressure for lots of speed on the downswing.

STEP 1

ALIGN YOUR SHOULDERS PARALLEL TO THE HILL. This is key to avoid digging into the hill. Play the ball toward the upper middle of your stance.

DO THIS

IF THE GRASS IS THICK OR YOUR BALL IS SITTING DOWN, CHOOSE A MORE-LOFTED CLUB. Just make sure you make a longer swing to compensate for the added loft. More loft means less distance.

UPHILL SLOPE

HOW TO HIT FROM AN UPHILL LIE

It is all in your setup. Keep in mind the upward slope of the hill will shoot the ball HIGHER THAN NORMAL.

STEP 2

SWING UP THE SLOPE with smooth acceleration through impact to a full finish. Swinging to a full finish will prevent deceleration.

STEP 1

ALIGN YOUR SHOULDERS PARALLEL TO THE HILL. This is key to avoid scooping or thinning the ball. Play the ball slightly back of center.

IF THE GRASS IS EXTRA DEEP, play the ball in the back of your stance off your right heel to ensure you get the club on the ball quickly.

DO THIS

DOWNHILL SLOPE

HOW TO HIT FROM A DOWNHILL LIE

It is all in your setup. Keep in mind the downward slope of the hill will promote a lower ball flight. So select a club with more loft to ensure getting the ball airborne.

STEP 2

SWING DOWN THE SLOPE with smooth acceleration through impact to avoid coming out of the shot.

WIND AND RAIN
MESSES UP MORE THAN YOUR HAIR

PLAYING THE WIND
when it's breezy, swing easy

STEP 1

Play the ball slightly back in your stance and choose one more club than usual to help reduce trajectory (keep it low).

STEP 2

If it is an extra windy day, widen your stance for more stability. A big backswing is not required. Remember, the extra club you selected in step 1 will get you to your destination.

STEP 3

Swing EASY through the ball. DO NOT TRY TO KILL IT. Think half-speed on the downswing. Finish with your hands low to keep the ball low.

WET LIES AND GOLF BOOT CAMP

NO ONE LIKES TO PLAY IN THE WIND AND RAIN, OR DO THEY?

One year I was invited to play golf in Ireland with the boys. Ten glorious days of golf, 36 holes on some days. It was early in my golfing career, so I was excited about the opportunity to explore foreign fairways and greens. I was warned to pack accordingly, as the weather would not be ideal; twenty-mile-an-hour winds with light mist was forecast. So I went to the golf store and bought the best rain gear money could buy, as well as rain gloves and an invert-proof umbrella.

The first day we played at Lahinch Golf Club, Lahinch, County Clare, Ireland. The weather was fierce: fifty-mile-an-hour winds with heavy rain. I couldn't believe we were actually going to tee it up in these dreadful hurricane-like conditions.

The boys explained that this is why they come to Ireland. Anything else wouldn't be as fun. So I went along with it and made some adjustments to my setup and swing tempo, to name a few.

Follow these steps to ensure you play your best the next time you get caught in hurricane-like conditions, and retreating to the cozy, dry clubhouse is not an option:

- When fairways are soggy due to heavy rainfall, the ball has a tendency to settle down in the grass. As a result, you'll tend to hit behind the ball or fat. To make matters worse, you'll feel like you're hitting out of the rough, and the ball will not have as much roll. SOLUTION: Select one club more than you normally would to ensure you do not swing too hard and to compensate for less roll.

- In your setup, play the ball more back than you normally would to ensure you catch the ball first. So for example, play the ball in the center of your stance with a wood or a middle iron rather than left of center.

- Now, just swing easy to keep the ball low. Finish your shots with a more-controlled, shorter finish to promote a lower ball flight.

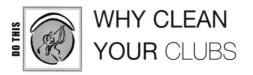

WHY CLEAN YOUR CLUBS

DO THIS

It is raining cats and dogs, and the mud is accumulating in the grooves of your club faces. What is a girl to do?

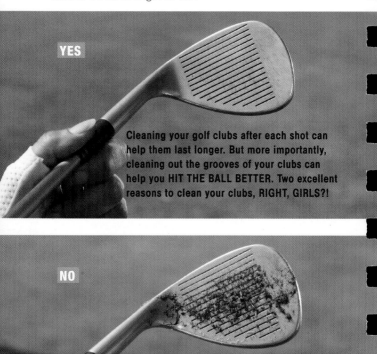

YES

Cleaning your golf clubs after each shot can help them last longer. But more importantly, cleaning out the grooves of your clubs can help you HIT THE BALL BETTER. Two excellent reasons to clean your clubs, RIGHT, GIRLS?!

NO

GEAR

You are playing a terrific round when the wind picks up and the raindrops start falling. You are not ready to head in, but you have no rain gear. Here is how to prepare the next time you get caught in the rain:

- **Always have an umbrella, and make sure it's not one of those wimpy ones!**

- **Rain gloves are a must. These are good ones to have in your bag.**

- **A good rain suit and a pair of waterproof shoes are a must.**

- **A rain hat is key. If you live in a cooler climate, get a hat that has a bit of insulation. If your head is warm, it tends to keep your whole body warmer.**

- **In cooler months, hand warmers and a pair of mittens for in-between shots are lovely.**

- **Stay focused, as if it were not raining. Don't let the elements make you rush or lose focus.**

MUDDY
PROPOSITION

When the lift, clean, and place rule
is not in effect, what is a girl to do?

ADVANCED

Mud on your ball? Keep these
points in mind. The ball won't
carry as far, and will most likely
veer off-line. Why? Simple, the ball is no longer
a perfect shape; it is covered with mud. The
key is to swing softer. The harder you swing,
the more off-line the ball will go due to the mud
factor. Take one more club than you normally
would to compensate for less distance.

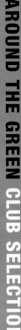

THE RIGHT CLUB
FOR THE JOB

Different shots require a different club. A long chip requires more roll, so a 9-, 8-, or 7-iron is a good choice. If there is little green and you need more height to land the ball softly with little roll, a lob or sand wedge is a good choice.

DO THIS

Get the ball on the green and rolling as soon as possible. Land the ball just on the green and let the ball roll to the hole.

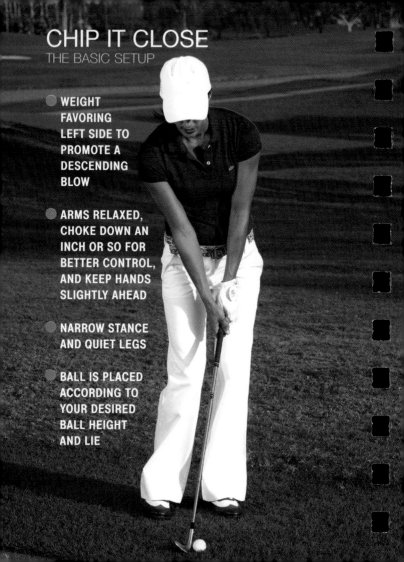

CHIP IT CLOSE
THE BASIC SETUP

- WEIGHT FAVORING LEFT SIDE TO PROMOTE A DESCENDING BLOW

- ARMS RELAXED, CHOKE DOWN AN INCH OR SO FOR BETTER CONTROL, AND KEEP HANDS SLIGHTLY AHEAD

- NARROW STANCE AND QUIET LEGS

- BALL IS PLACED ACCORDING TO YOUR DESIRED BALL HEIGHT AND LIE

The difference between a CHIP and a PITCH is simple. With a CHIP, the ball has minimal air-time and more roll time. With a PITCH, there is more air-time required to carry the ball to the landing area. A CHIP typically is just off the green, on the fringe or in the rough. A PITCH, typically is from the fairway or from the rough.

PITCH IT CLOSE
THE BASIC SETUP

- MORE WRIST HINGE, ARM AND HAND ACTION IS REQUIRED IN A PITCH SHOT

- LEGS MORE ACTIVE; YOUR HIPS TURN SLIGHTLY THROUGH A PITCH SHOT

- BALL IS PLACED ACCORDING TO YOUR DESIRED BALL HEIGHT AND LIE

GOOD LIE

VERSUS

BAD LIE

LIE ASSESSMENT
KNOW WHAT YOU CAN DO

Different shots require different clubs, and different lies require different approaches. Be creative and follow these guidelines to get it close.

SHOTS WITH A GOOD LIE

- utilize the roll/ratio formula
- try the flop shot with this lie
- low running shots with PW-7 irons
- loose grip better
- good tempo a must

SHOTS WITH A BAD LIE

- requires a steeper angle of attack with a shorter follow-through
- requires more wrist hinge
- ball comes out hotter, more roll, less spin
- sand wedge, lob wedge, or PW best bet
- hold the club more firmly out of the rough so it doesn't twist in your hands at contact
- 60 percent of weight on front foot to encourage a steeper angle of attack
- good tempo a must; don't chop at the ball

HOW TO CHIP IT CLOSE

I often see players take a mammoth backswing with lots of wrist hinge, to chip the ball 20 yards. They typically end up decelerating and "chunking" the shot. A chip requires more shoulder action than arms and hands action. Your arms and hands are quiet through the shot. The number one element of a chip—HIT DOWN ON THE BALL. If you don't, you will hit the ball thin and will lack distance control.

STEP 1

Pick your intermediate target. In this photo, the target is an area inside the pink circle. Choose the appropriate club, depending on the distance you need the ball to carry and roll.

Set up square to the target.

This is enough backswing for a 10- to 20-yard chip.

STEP 2

Start the backswing with your shoulders using an even tempo. Not too fast; there is no rush. The ball is not going anywhere.

Hands remain ahead through the shot. DON'T try to scoop or lift the ball, the loft of the club does that all by itself. ----▶

STEP 3

On the downswing your only thought should be to hit down on the back of the ball with steady acceleration. It is not a jab. Tempo is key on the downswing as much as the backswing. HEAD IS VERY QUIET.

CHIP - LOW RUNNER
BE THE BALL, FEEL THE SHOT, AND GET IT CLOSE!

Maintain the triangle through the shot.

REMEMBER this is more of a shoulder move not a hands and arms move.

Hands slightly ahead.

For a low runner, play the ball back in your stance.

KEY POINTS to determine where to land the ball

YES

Speed of the greens. Are they rolling fast or slow?

Check the slope. Is the green sloping downhill or uphill? Sometimes landing on the fringe is a better choice for a downhill slope.

Is the green hard or soft? With a softer green, you can be more aggressive and go for the pin. On a harder green, anticipate more roll.

DO THIS

IF THE ROUGH IS SUPER TOUGH, make an upright backswing with lots of wrist hinge. On the downswing hit down into the grass firmly. Do not expect a big finish with this shot.

GREENSIDE ROUGH
LOFTY IDEAS WORK BEST

STEP 1

USE YOUR LOB OR SAND WEDGE. Tall grass tends to close the face, so you need loft to help you. Play the ball back in your stance, off your right toe.

STEP 2

Take a normal chipping stroke, and the ball should pop onto the green. The ball will roll more because there is more grass between you and the ball, so pick the right landing spot.

CHIP-LOB SHOT
IF YOU HAVE LITTLE GREEN TO WORK WITH AND
NEED A HIGH SOFT SHOT, HERE'S WHAT TO DO.

STEP 1

Select your lob or
sand wedge. Play the
ball in the center or
just ahead of center.
Setup is slightly open,
meaning that my body
is lined up left of the
flag. Pick your landing
spot. The circle is my
landing spot.

grip down on
the club for
more control

STEP 2

A steeper backswing with wrist hinge is key here. The length of the backswing is determined by the length of the shot. Don't over-think the backswing. This is a feel shot, so trust your swing!

clubface pointing to the sky, indicating quiet hands through the shot

STEP 3

Hands stay low through impact, letting the loft of the club do the work. Steady acceleration always, girls!

leading edge at
equator of ball

ADVANCED

CHIP **FROM THE COLLAR**

Setup is the same as a chip shot. The ball is ahead
of center, and your weight favors the left side. The
only difference is that, instead of hitting down, you
need to stroke the ball like a putt. Play a sand or
pitching wedge on the equator of the ball. You want
the club's leading edge to strike the center of the ball.

ANOTHER OPTION—TRY A HYBRID OR FAIRWAY
WOOD, MY MOTHER'S FAVORITE FROM THE
ROUGH AND FRINGE. ⟶

CHIP - FAIRWAY WOOD

A GREAT CHOICE, MOM. The sole of the club is more forgiving out of the rough, and the loft helps get the ball up and on the green. From there it rolls like a putt or a low running chip. ONLY TRY THIS SHOT IF THE BALL IS ON THE FRINGE OR SITTING UP IN THE ROUGH.

STEP 1

GRIP DOWN on the shaft for more control. Position the ball back in your stance.

STEP 2

KEEPING THE TRIANGLE and hands ahead like a normal chip shot, execute with steady acceleration.

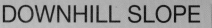

DOWNHILL SLOPE
PITCH FROM A DOWNHILL LIE

STEP 1

ALIGN YOUR SHOULDERS PARALLEL TO THE HILL. Your weight should favor your downhill leg. Play the ball right of center to encourage a clean strike.

DO THIS

IF THE GRASS IS EXTRA DEEP, play the ball in the back of your stance off your right heel to ensure you get the club on the ball quickly.

It is all in your setup. Keep in mind the downward slope of the hill will promote a lower ball flight. So select a club with more loft to ensure getting the ball airborne.

STEP 2

SWING DOWN THE SLOPE with smooth acceleration through impact to avoid coming out of the shot.

UPHILL SLOPE
PITCH FROM AN UPHILL LIE

STEP 1

ALIGN YOUR SHOULDERS TO THE HILL. Tilt your shoulders parallel to the hill so that most of your weight is on the downhill leg. This is key to avoid digging into the hill. Play the ball toward the middle of your stance. Take a slightly wider stance for stability.

DO THIS

IF THE GRASS IS SUPER THICK or your ball is sitting down, use a sand wedge to help penetrate the grass easier.

It is all in your setup. Keep in mind the upward slope of the hill will shoot the ball almost straight up with little roll.

STEP 2
SWING UP THE SLOPE with smooth acceleration through impact to a full finish.

THE ROLL RATIO FORMULA

<--- LOB WEDGE

<--- SAND WEDGE

<--- PITCHING WEDGE

CARRY TO ROLL RATIO

CLUB SELECTION

- **LOB WEDGE 3:1 RATIO**
  flies 3 times as far as it rolls

- **SAND WEDGE 2:1 RATIO**
  flies twice as far as it rolls

- **PITCHING WEDGE 1:2 ratio**
  rolls 2 times as far as it flies

- **9 iron 1:3 ratio**
  rolls 3 times as far as it flies

- **8 iron 1:4 ratio**
  rolls 4 times as far as it flies

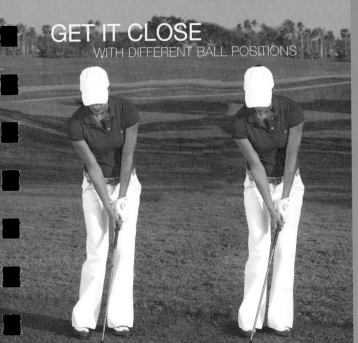

GET IT CLOSE
WITH DIFFERENT BALL POSITIONS

For a **LOW SHOT** where the ball rolls to the hole, play the ball back in your stance. Shown right.

For a shot that has a **MID-TRAJECTORY**, play the ball in the center of your stance. Shown left.

For a **HIGH, SOFT SHOT** that has more carry and less roll, play the ball ahead of center in your stance. Not shown.

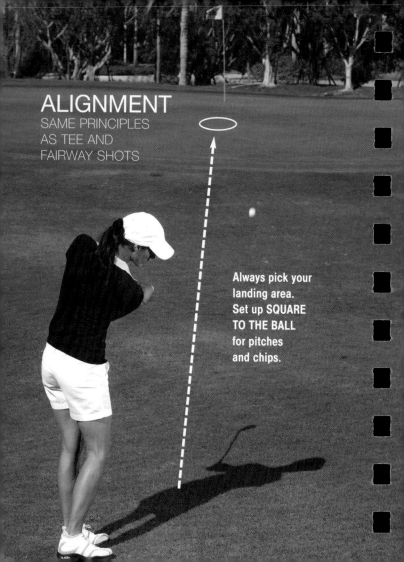

ALIGNMENT
SAME PRINCIPLES
AS TEE AND
FAIRWAY SHOTS

Always pick your
landing area.
Set up SQUARE
TO THE BALL
for pitches
and chips.

ALIGNMENT
FOR HIGH, SOFT SHOTS

EXCEPT for high, soft shots which require more of an **OPEN STANCE AND CLUBFACE.**

Open your stance and clubface for a high, soft shot.

BAD-SHOT FIXES
MAIN CAUSES OF
MISSED CHIPS
AND PITCHES

① **ALIGNMENT** High soft shots

② **DISTANCE CONTROL** Can't seem to get it close?

③ **DIRECTIONALLY CHALLENGED** Flipping, scooping, decelerating, wrist action, and take-away

ALIGNMENT FOR HIGH, SOFT SHOT Body lines left of target to promote an out-to-in path.

① ALIGNMENT

I often see a player aligning too far right or directly at the hole for high, soft shots. Instead, you need a slightly open stance, and you need to aim just left of the hole. Why? The ball will have a tendency to spin right when it lands because of the open setup and open clubface.

② DISTANCE CONTROL

A simple way to control your distance from 100 yards and in is to visualize a clock. Know what your distances are from 9-3, 8-4, and 10-2.

My 9-3 distance with a pitching wedge is 80 yards.
KNOW YOUR DISTANCE.

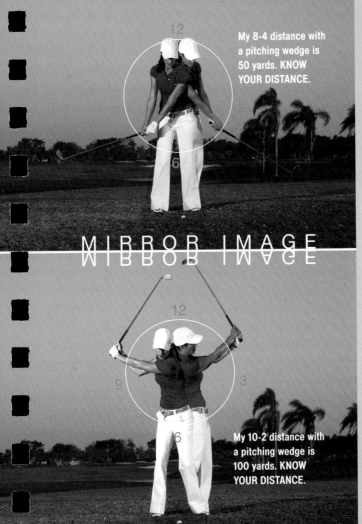

My 8-4 distance with a pitching wedge is 50 yards. KNOW YOUR DISTANCE.

My 10-2 distance with a pitching wedge is 100 yards. KNOW YOUR DISTANCE.

MIRROR IMAGE

③ DIRECTIONALLY CHALLENGED
scoop, flipped, cupped

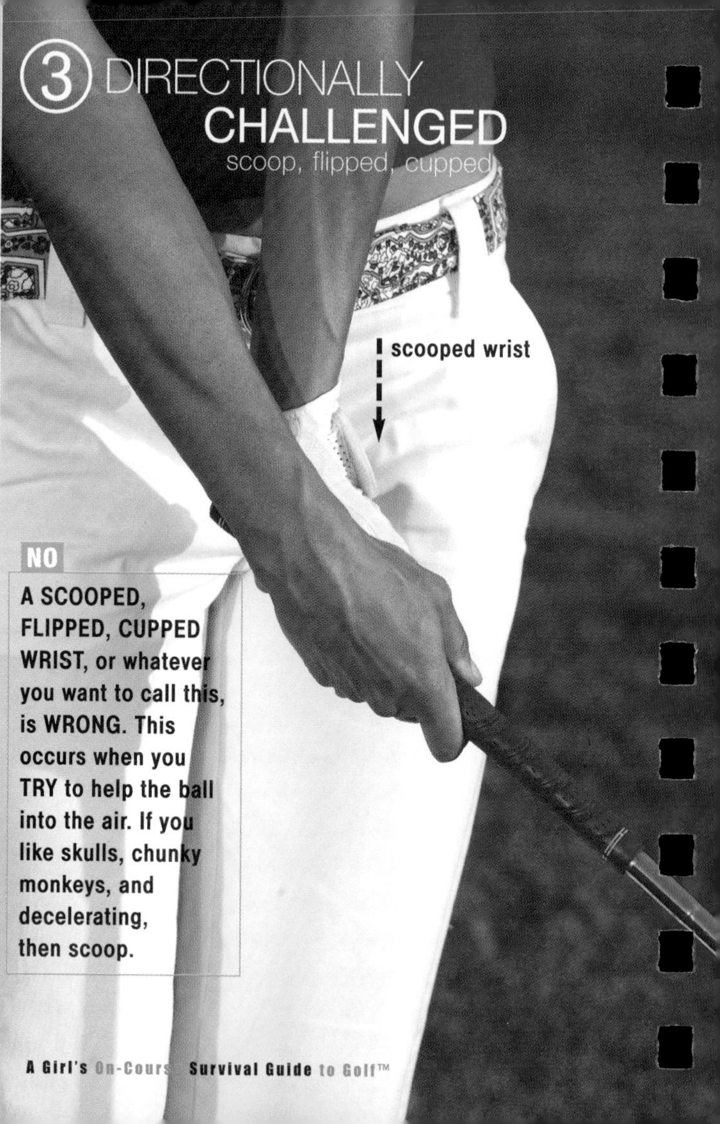

↓ scooped wrist

NO

A SCOOPED, FLIPPED, CUPPED WRIST, or whatever you want to call this, is WRONG. This occurs when you TRY to help the ball into the air. If you like skulls, chunky monkeys, and decelerating, then scoop.

HINGE AND HOLD for consistent trajectory and feel

YES

On your downswing, your hands LEAD THE WAY. This allows for a descending blow that promotes a crisp shot.

③ DIRECTIONALLY
CHALLENGED
good wrist action

hands rolled →

YES

For a medium pitch, a 50-yard shot, for example, roll your hands and release. Do not hold on and try to guide the shot to the hole.

YES

For a short pitch, this is good release. My hands haven't rolled because I do not need to carry the ball too far. A 20- to 30-yard pitch, for example.

③ DIRECTIONALLY CHALLENGED
poor take-away

YES

PERFECT PATH! MY TAKE-AWAY IS PARALLEL TO THE TARGET LINE This ensures that the clubhead returns to square through impact while maintaining the club's loft.

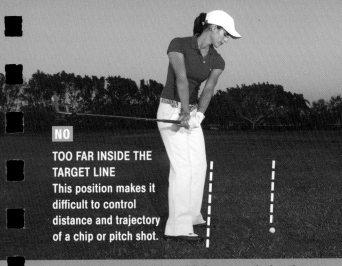

NO

TOO FAR INSIDE THE TARGET LINE
This position makes it difficult to control distance and trajectory of a chip or pitch shot.

KEEP YOUR CLUBFACE SQUARE. Do not manipulate the clubface. It will be VERY difficult to square the face through impact, thus causing erratic shots.

closed face

open face

KEY POINT

KEY POINTS
FOR BUNKER SETUP

- AN OPEN STANCE, MEANING YOUR FEET, HIPS, AND SHOULDERS ARE AIMED LEFT OF THE TARGET, WHICH PROMOTES AN OUT-TO-IN SWING PATH.

- SET YOUR CLUBFACE OPEN TO UTILIZE THE BOUNCE (SOLE) OF THE CLUB.

- BALL POSITION IS JUST LEFT OF CENTER.

BE SURE TO HINGE YOUR WRISTS IN THE BACKSWING.

RELEASE THROUGH THE SAND ON A SLIGHT OUT-TO-IN PATH, MAKING SURE TO CATCH SAND FIRST. MOST IMPORTANTLY, ACCELERATE THROUGH THE SHOT.

185

YES

For more roll, hit at least 3-4 inches behind the ball. The more sand you take the less backspin.

3-4 inches behind for more roll

WHERE AND HOW MUCH
MORE SAND means LESS SPIN

The key to a sand shot is to MAKE SURE YOU TAKE SAND. It is not a sand shot if you pick the ball cleanly. THE SAND PROPELS THE BALL OUT OF THE BUNKER. Also, the texture of the sand plays a role. As a general rule, the fluffier or finer the sand, the more the clubhead will dig into the sand. Therefore a more-open clubface is needed to let the bounce of the club do its job. With a coarse, heavier sand, the clubhead will tend to bounce off the surface. Therefore a more-square clubface at address is needed so the club can dig into the sand.

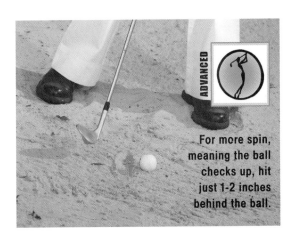

ADVANCED

For more spin, meaning the ball checks up, hit just 1-2 inches behind the ball.

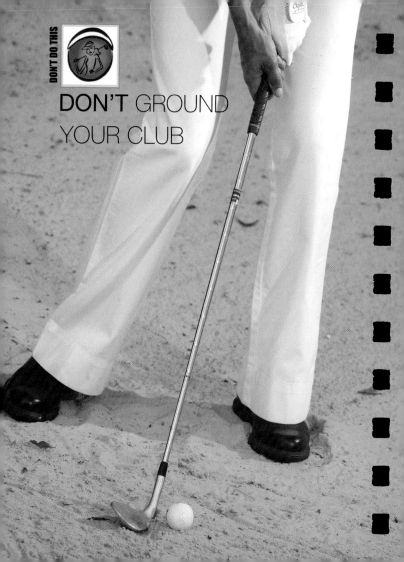

DON'T DO THIS

DON'T GROUND
YOUR CLUB

RULES

DO HOVER YOUR CLUB

A BOUNCE lies along the back edge of the sole of the club. It sits lower than the leading edge, making it easier to travel through the sand.

LEADING EDGE

BOUNCE

A SANDWICH?
NO, A SAND WEDGE!

The reason why we use a sand wedge is its unique design. The purpose of bounce is to help the club cut through the sand more easily. The more bounce a wedge has, the more its sole will tend to get through the sand, which helps to get the ball up and out, and, hopefully, close to the hole.

Who the heck invented this odd, yet very useful club?

Gene Sarazen was the first golfer to win the modern career grand slam (victories in each of golf's four professional majors), and he was was inducted into the World Golf Hall of Fame in 1974. His accomplishments on the course were remarkable, but Sarazen is also famous for an off-course accomplishment: he invented the modern sand wedge. Sarazen invented the modern sand wedge in 1930. He called it the sand iron.

Prior to Sarazen's invention, players used a variety of clubs designed to get them out of trouble. "Spoon" clubs offered varying degrees of loft and allowed players to scoop their ball out of sand traps and deep rough. These methods were outlawed in 1931, so Sarazen designed his sand wedge with a straight face with extra lead to the front edge of the club face, allowing it to cut through the sand more smoothly. After he won the 1932 British and U.S. Opens with the help of his new club, its popularity quickly grew.

Ball position slightly ahead of center and clubface square.

STEP 1

YOUR STANCE IS SLIGHTLY OPEN BUT NOT AS MUCH AS A NORMAL BUNKER SHOT. Select either a SW, PW, or even a 9-iron, depending on the distance you need to carry to the green.

192

LONG
GREENSIDE
BUNKERS

STEP 2

A BIG BACKSWING IS
KEY HERE, but tempo
is even more important.
A controlled swing with
head still is a must.
You need steady
acceleration to propel
the ball 30-40 yards to
the green.

THE BURIED LIE
a.k.a. THE FRIED EGG

STEP 1

TO GET THE BALL OUT, A VERTICAL ANGLE OF ATTACK IS REQUIRED, so set up with an open stance to encourage a steep out-to-in path. Weight is on your left side, with a square clubface at address.

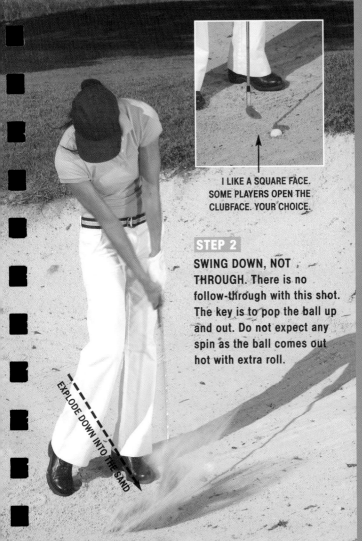

I LIKE A SQUARE FACE. SOME PLAYERS OPEN THE CLUBFACE. YOUR CHOICE.

STEP 2

SWING DOWN, NOT THROUGH. There is no follow-through with this shot. The key is to pop the ball up and out. Do not expect any spin as the ball comes out hot with extra roll.

EXPLODE DOWN INTO THE SAND

195

STEP 1

Position the ball ahead of center. Tilt your spine with the slope and open your stance. On the backswing cock your wrists fully.

THE UPHILL LIE
ALL IN THE SETUP

STEP 2

You want to hit into the hill and pop the ball out. Don't try to scoop the ball out. Follow-through will be minimal, if any.

RULES

BALL IDENTIFICATION. In a bunker, you are not allowed to pick up your ball for identification; otherwise you will incur a one-stroke penalty.

THE DOWNHILL LIE
ALL IN THE SETUP

STEP 1

Tilt your spine with the slope and
open your stance and clubface.
Position the ball back of center. Your
weight should favor your left side
to discourage hitting too much sand.

STEP 2

Swing down the slope and keep your weight moving forward. The ball will have minimal spin, if any, and will come out of the bunker low.

HIT DOWN ALONG THE SLOPE

NO GREEN AND SERIOUSLY CLOSE TO THE EDGE

Need to get the ball out with some immediate height. Follow these steps.

STEP 1

Play the ball just ahead of center, and open your stance and clubface.

Swing down along stance line, an out-to-in path.

STEP 2

Make a three-quarter backswing with lots of wrist hinge. Hit two inches behind the ball and ACCELERATE through the shot. The keys to this shot—lots of sand, and good acceleration. On your follow-through, the clubface remains open, producing a high, soft shot.

WHAT THE HECK IS A LIP?

STEP 1

An awkward shot, so set yourself as best you can for stability. If your feet are not level, be sure to set yourself parallel to the slope. Similar to an uphill lie setup. Grip down on the shaft with a square clubface at address.

A LIP IS WHERE THE GRASS MEETS THE SAND IN A BUNKER. Sometimes your ball sits under this lip; not a pretty sight. ●●●●●●●●●●➤

STEP 2

With just a half-backswing and good wrist hinge, drive the clubhead down into the sand just behind the ball. There will be no follow-through because you are hitting into the lip. Your ball should pop up and out.

ETIQUETTE

YES-YES-YES

NO-NO-NO

10-SECOND RULE

FOR A BALL ON THE EDGE OF A HOLE.
If a ball comes to rest on the edge of
a hole, you can wait for 10 seconds.
If the ball drops within this time frame
congratulations. If it falls after the 10
seconds or not at all, better luck next
time. Add another stroke.

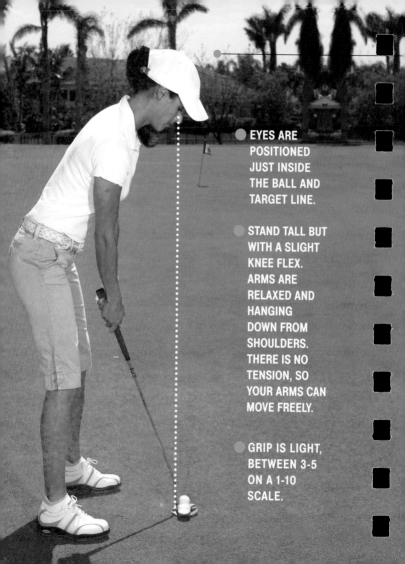

EYES ARE POSITIONED JUST INSIDE THE BALL AND TARGET LINE.

STAND TALL BUT WITH A SLIGHT KNEE FLEX. ARMS ARE RELAXED AND HANGING DOWN FROM SHOULDERS. THERE IS NO TENSION, SO YOUR ARMS CAN MOVE FREELY.

GRIP IS LIGHT, BETWEEN 3-5 ON A 1-10 SCALE.

KEY POINTS FOR
GOOD POSTURE

There are three key components to a putt: POSTURE, AIM, and SPEED. Get these right and you'll be one-putting.

NOT-SO-GOOD POSTURE

NO

AVOID POSTURE THAT RESULTS IN FLYING ELBOWS. TENSION IS SURE TO CREEP INTO THIS SETUP.

ALSO, IF YOU ARE BENT OVER TOO MUCH, YOUR EYES WILL MOVE OUTSIDE THE TARGET LINE, WHICH WILL EFFECT YOUR AIM.

STEP 1

READ THE GREEN

Read for break and slope.
Give yourself enough room
to see the break and slope.
Do not read the green too
close to the hole.

STEP 2

TAKE PRACTICE STROKES

From behind the ball you
can see the line better. It
also sends a signal to your
brain about the speed.

PRE-PUTT ROUTINE

A pre-shot routine is as important on the putting
surface as it is on the tee or in the fairway. It
keeps you focused on the task at hand—making
the putt without distraction.

STEP 3

STEP INTO THE BALL AND AIM THE CLUBFACE
When aiming, it is best to pick an intermediate target. It is easier to aim for a spot 2 feet in front of you than 15 feet.

STEP 4

TAKE YOUR STANCE
Set yourself by making sure your feet, hips, and shoulders are parallel to the putt's target line.

STEP 5
GO!

DISTANCE CONTROL
SAME LENGTH BACK AND THROUGH

YES

A good method of regulating distance is to mirror your back stroke and forward stroke with consistent tempo.

MENTAL

TRY THIS and make more putts:
Commit to holding your putting finish
for three seconds without peeking.

YES

MAINTAIN THE TRIANGLE. The putting stroke is shoulders and arms working together as one piece. Keep your hands quiet through the stroke.

YES

TEMPO IS KEY, especially under pressure. Find your rhythm and keep it with you, always.

PUTT AIM HIGH

A common mistake I see players make is not playing enough break. The ball misses on the low side, a.k.a. amateur side, SO WHEN READING A PUTT, PICK YOUR POINT OF ENTRY where you think the ball will begin to drop. Remember the ball usually breaks the most just at the hole, so give your putt a chance and putt on the high side, a.k.a. pro side.

Visualize your point of entry

YES

The key to breaking putts is speed. You need to get the ball to the breaking point, and then the ball should fall to the hole.

SHORT PUTTS
PUTTER TO THE HOLE

Key to short putts is
commitment. Pick your line,
set up to the ball, and trust it.
When you do not trust your line,
missed putts happen.

DO THIS

Focus on target, not the ball.
For short putts, pick a spot
inside the hole, and visualize
your ball hitting that spot.

LONG PUTTS
LAG IT CLOSE EVERY TIME

It is key to read the break in long putts. If you miss the line, it only makes it more difficult to 2-putt. Pay special attention to the last 5 feet to determine the ball's entry point.

YES

LAG THE LONG PUTTS
Long putts require the same technique as the short ones. They are just longer. The same tempo and distance control is required. **THE OBJECT IS TO GET YOUR BALL IN THE 3-FOOT CIRCLE.**

- CHECK THE GRAIN. If down grain, expect more roll. Against the grain, expect less roll.
- PICK AN INTERMEDIATE TARGET about halfway to the hole, then aim for that spot.
- CHECK THE SLOPE. Look at the hole; which side is higher? Visualize the fall line. If you poured a bucket of water, where would the water fall.
- PUTT TO A 3-FOOT CIRCLE to ensure a 2-putt.

3-ft circle

YES

CHECK YOUR POSTURE. Drop a ball from your eye to the ground. If it lands anywhere inside the ball or just at it, you're OK. Otherwise check your setup. You are either too close or too far from the ball.

BAD-SHOT FIXES
MAIN CAUSES OF
MISSED PUTTS

① **ALIGNMENT** Key with putts too, not only setting up to the line but also trusting the line.

② **SWING PATH** Too inside or too outside affects the line.

③ **DISTANCE CONTROL** If you do not get the ball to the hole, you'll never have a chance. On the flip side, if the ball goes 5 feet past the hole, it is a tester coming back.

NEVER WALK IN ANOTHER PLAYER'S LINE. THIS IS THE GOLDEN RULE OF ETIQUETTE.

NO PEEKING !!

If you peek, a few things will happen: your ball will go off-line, your putter will not make solid contact, and you will most likely miss the putt. If you find yourself peeking—PUTT A FEW WITH YOUR EYES CLOSED—it is all about trusting your line and speed.

① ALIGNMENT

YES

← Always pick a blade of grass or some spot to set your clubface that is on the line of your putt. This ensures your alignment is correct at address.

② SWING PATH

Straight back and through
on the short putts.

YES

Straight back and straight through
is key on short putts.

Square is the name of the game in putting.
If at address your square, but then take the
club too inside or too outside, you will need
to manipulate the clubface to get it square
again through impact.

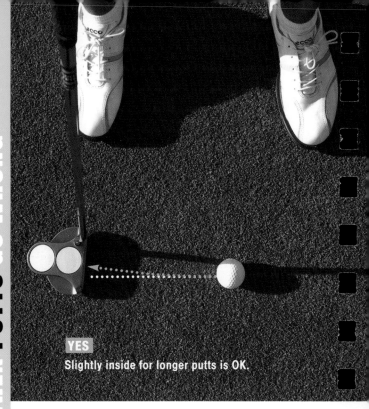

YES

Slightly inside for longer putts is OK.

② SWING PATH
Inside the target line

NO
This path is too inside.

For longer putts, the club will naturally move to the inside slightly, simply because your shoulders are more active on longer putts.

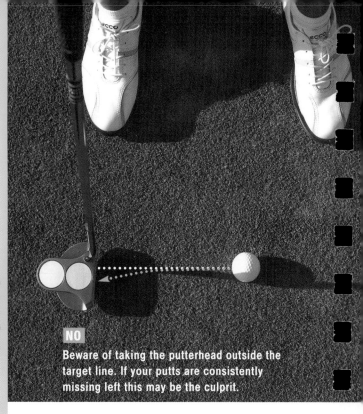

NO
Beware of taking the putterhead outside the target line. If your putts are consistently missing left this may be the culprit.

(2) SWING PATH
outside the target line

③ DISTANCE CONTROL
a.k.a. speed

NO
Don't force square, my nemisis still.

NO
Don't allow the wrist to cup or break through impact—A **DISTANCE CONTROL KILLER.**

WHEN PUTTS GO WRONG

YES

For more consistency, make sure your backstroke is the same as your forward stroke.

READING THE GREEN

The grain and type of grass influence the way the ball rolls. Before you set up to your putt, keep these simple rules in mind:

● The greens are typically quicker early in the day, as the greens are just cut, and slower at the end of the day, as the grass has grown through the day.

● Grain is always a factor. Check the cup and look for the brown shaggy side, that is the direction the grain is growing. So if you are putting with the grain, your putt will roll faster. Against the grain, your ball will roll slower.

● Water affects the grain. The ball tends to break toward bodies of water. So if there is a lake, expect the ball to break that way.

● Believe it or not, wind plays a role, especially a strong wind. The ball is light, so if it is a really windy day and you are putting into the wind, expect the ball to roll slower, and vice versa.

FEAR OF WATER SYNDROME
ALWAYS DIRECT YOUR ENERGIES TOWARD THE TARGET.

If you fear the water, you will go in the water. Instead, forget the water, and focus on, for example, the three palm trees over the water as your target.

MENTAL

- CONCENTRATE ON THE RIGHT THINGS, like target, yardage, club selection, and feel of the shot. Do not think about mechanics, fixating on the ball, or where you DO NOT want to hit the ball.

- DO KNOW YOUR YARDAGES WITH EACH CLUB, and know what the yardage is to the flagstick and front of the green. Sometimes hitting to the front of the green and letting the ball roll to the hole is a wiser decision.

- DON'T PLAY SHOTS YOU HAVE NOT PRACTICED, especially in competition.

- DON'T BE A HERO. Go for it only if you can make the shot 8 out of 10 times.

- SOMETIMES A DRIVER ISN'T THE BEST CHOICE. If you rip your driver and end up in the fairway bunker, where's the advantage? Hit a 3-wood instead.

- FOR FIRST-TEE JITTERS, BREATHE AND BREATHE SLOWLY. If for some reason your first hole wasn't how you envisioned, don't worry, you have 17 more to go.

- IF YOU DO GET INTO TROUBLE, GET OUT IN ONE SHOT. Don't compound the issue with mistake after mistake. AVOID THE SNOWMAN.

- IF YOU ARE HAVING ONE OF THOSE DAYS, JUST STICK WITH IT AND STAY IN THE PRESENT. You will have the best chance at turning your game around.

YES

BRING WHOLESOME
SANDWICHES AND FRUIT
FROM HOME, OR OPT FOR A
KOSHER ALL-BEEF HOT DOG.

GOOD NUTRITION
ORGANIC AND NO TRANS FATS

YES ORGANIC AND HIGH IN PROTEIN.

YES GREAT FILLER AND HIGH IN ANTIOXIDANTS AND PROTEIN.

PICK THE RIGHT SNACK
for mental clarity and high energy

NO BAD CHOICE—FULL OF NASTY SUGARS SUCH AS CORN SYRUP AND BAD OILS SUCH AS PALM KERNEL OIL. NOT TO MENTION THE CHEMICALS!

PROTEIN BARS

GET OUT OF **TROUBLE**

EGO, STEP ASIDE

Uh-Oh! A missed tee shot into the woods. Now what?! Unless you're Annika, let your ego rest. Take the easiest route back out to the fairway.

Do, however, go for it if you feel
100 percent confident that you can
make a particular shot. If there is ZERO
doubt, then go ahead, "GO FOR IT!"

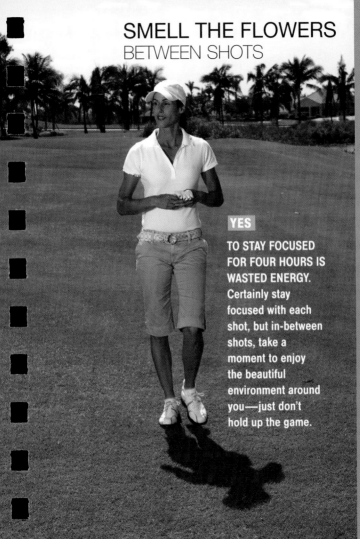

SMELL THE FLOWERS
BETWEEN SHOTS

YES

TO STAY FOCUSED FOR FOUR HOURS IS WASTED ENERGY. Certainly stay focused with each shot, but in-between shots, take a moment to enjoy the beautiful environment around you—just don't hold up the game.

TENSION IS NOT A GIRL'S BEST FRIEND

MENTAL

Tension is an issue we all face. It affects everything from shot success to mental stamina. To alleviate tension, especially after a bad shot:

- try deep breathing
- sing to yourself
- smell the flowers between shots
- hum
- break a pattern, do something out of character (for example, if you are shy, be more outgoing that day)
- tell jokes, laugh

HOW TO COPE AFTER
THE 10TH #$$@!!?? SHOT

LAUGH. IT IS THE BEST MEDICINE WHEN THINGS ARE GOING HAYWIRE. Here are some funny jokes, **WHEN ALL ELSE FAILS.**

A hack golfer spends a day at a plush country club, playing golf, enjoying the luxury of a complimentary caddy. Being a hack golfer, he plays poorly all day. Round about the 18th hole, he spots a lake off to the left of the fairway. He looks at the caddy and says, "I've played so poorly all day; I think I'm going to go drown myself in that lake."

The caddy looks back at him and says, "I don't think you could keep your head down that long."

I was playing this hole one time with a senior citizen and just as he was about ready to hit his tee shot he noticed a funeral procession approaching. He took off his hat, put it over his heart, and stood silently and watched the procession go by until it disappeared. I said, "That's really nice of you. Do you always do that when a funeral goes by?" He said, "No, not usually, but it's the least I could do in this case. I was married to the woman for 40 years!"

After a particularly poor game of golf, a popular club member skipped the clubhouse and started to go home. As he was walking to the parking lot to get his car, a policeman stopped

Cont'd next page ☞

him and asked, "Did you tee off on the sixteenth hole about twenty minutes ago?"

"Yes," the golfer responded.

"Did you happen to hook your ball so that it went over the trees and off the course?"

"Yes, I did. How did you know?" he asked.

"Well," said the policeman very seriously, "Your ball flew out onto the highway and crashed through a driver's windshield. The car went out of control, crashing into five other cars and a fire truck. The fire truck couldn't make it to the fire, and the building burned down. So, what are you going to do about it?" The golfer thought it over carefully and responded . . .

"I think I'll close my stance a little bit, tighten my grip and lower my right thumb."

A golfer is in a competitive match with a friend, who is ahead by a couple of strokes. The golfer says to himself, "I'd give anything to sink this next putt." A stranger walks up to him and whispers, "Would you give up a fourth of your sex life?"

The golfer thinks the man is crazy and that his answer will be meaningless. At the same time he thinks this might be a good women, so he says, "Okay," and sinks the putt.

Two holes later he mumbles to himself, "Boy, if I could only get an eagle on this hole." The same stranger moves to his side and says, "Would it be worth another fourth of your sex life?"

The golfer shrugs and says, "Sure." He makes an eagle. On the final hole, the golfer needs yet another eagle to win. Though he says nothing, the stranger moves to his side and says, "Would you be willing to give up the rest of your sex life to win this match?"

The golfer says, "Certainly!" He makes the eagle.
As the golfer walks to the club house, the stranger walks alongside and says, "You know, I've really not been fair with you because you don't know who I am. I'm the devil, and from now on you will have no sex life."

"Nice to meet you," says the golfer. "My name's... Father O'Malley."

Three friends were on the front nine one day and the group ahead of them were playing slow, terrible golf and weren't gesturing for a play-through. After several holes of this agonizingly slow golf the three friends began to get very impatient, each muttering his own curses upon the group ahead of them.

Soon the Marshall came about, and was hailed down by them shouting, "We're sick of being held up by these yahoos ahead of us who won't allow us to play through!" The Marshall stated,

Cont'd next page ☞

"I'm sorry, gentlemen, I know they're playing slowly, but those men are both deaf and blind."

The first friend cried, "Oh, I'm so sorry for yelling and for the bad things I was thinking about them."

The second friend cried, "I'm sorry as well. Maybe we can buy them a round of drinks in the clubhouse." The third friend muttered, "Why can't they play at night?"

There was a golf course that specialized in senior citizen caddies. After completing a round, the starter asked one golfer, "So, how did the caddie work out?" The man replied, "He was nice enough, but he couldn't see far enough to follow the ball." "I'm sorry," said the starter, "Come back next week, and I'll be sure you get a caddie that can see far enough."

The next week the man showed up and the starter introduced him to his eighty-year-old caddie. "Are you sure he can see?" asked the man. "Absolutely," said the starter. So off they went to the first tee. The man hit his drive and said to the caddie, "Did you see that?" "I sure did," came the reply. They walked together down the fairway and the man said to the caddie, "Well, where did my ball go?" The caddie replied, "I forget!"

The golfer hit his drive into the adjacent water hazard on the first hole. He walked over to look for his ball and saw it about six feet out from the shore in shallow water. He took his ball retriever from his bag, extended it and reached out into the water and got his ball. As he was drying it off, he heard a voice speak to him.

"Hey, mister," the voice said. He looked around and saw no one. He started back to drop his ball along the ball's line of flight as it went into the hazard. "Hey, mister," the voice said again.

He looked down amongst the weeds and grass growing by the water and saw a frog. This time he was looking at the frog when it said, "Hey, mister." "Yeah? What do you want, frog?" he asked. "Mister, I'm really a beautiful princess but a wicked witch has put a spell on me and turned me into an ugly frog. If you will pick me up and kiss me, I'll turn back into a beautiful princess. Then you can take me home and we'll make wild passionate love for hours," the frog said.

The man reached down, picked the frog up and put it in his windbreaker pocket. He walked a few yards back down the fairway and dropped his ball preparing for his third shot. "Hey, mister," the frog called, "aren't you going to kiss me?" The man took a couple of practice swings with his three-wood and then hit the ball onto the par four green. Walking on towards the green, he said, "No, I'm not going to kiss you. At my age I'd rather have a talking frog."

Jim and Bob were golfing one fine day, when Jim, an avid golfer, slices his ball deep into a wooded ravine. Jim takes his 8 iron and proceeds down the embankment into the ravine, in search of his lost ball. The brush is quite thick, but Jim searches diligently for his errant ball. Suddenly Jim spots something shiny. As he nears the location of the shiny object,

Cont'd next page ☞

Jim realizes that it is an eight iron in the hands of a skeleton laying near an old golf ball. Jim excitedly calls for his partner Bob. "Hey Bob, come here, I got trouble down here."

Bob comes running over to the edge of the ravine and calls out to Jim, "What's the matter Jim?" Jim shouts back in a nervous voice, "Bring me my 7 iron. You can't get out of here with an 8."

Two long time golfers were standing overlooking the river getting ready to hit their shots. One golfer looked to the other and said, "Look at those idiots fishin' in the rain."

Two guys at a convention get totally drunk the night before a big golf match. During the match the two half-bombed characters manage to stay even with their opponents through seventeen holes. On the eighteenth, by some miracle, they are in a position to win the match if one of them can sink his seven foot putt.

The man sets up to putt with his feet wide apart. He draws his putter back. Just then a big black dog, chasing a squirrel, comes running across the green, the dog goes right between the guy's legs, and out the other side and runs off the green. The guy never flinches but strokes the ball into the hole for the win!

His partner goes wild shouting "I have never seen such total concentration. How you managed to drop that putt with that dog running between your legs . . ." "Oh," says his partner, "Was that a REAL DOG!?!"

THE LAWS OF GOLF

1. If you really want to get better at golf, go back and take it up at a much earlier age.

2. The game of golf is 90% mental and 10% mental.

3. Since bad shots come in groups of three, a fourth bad shot is actually the beginning of the next group of three.

4. When you look up, causing an awful shot, you will always look down again at exactly the moment when you ought to

start watching the ball if you ever want to see it again.

5. If it ain't broke, try changing your grip.

6. No matter how bad you are playing, it is always possible to play worse.

7. Never try to keep more than 300 separate thoughts in your mind during your swing.

8. When your shot has to carry over a water hazard, you can either hit one more club or two more balls.

9. If you're afraid a full shot might reach the green while the foursome ahead of you is still putting out, you have two options: you can immediately shank a lay-up, or you can wait until the green is clear and top a ball halfway there.

10. The less skilled the player, the more likely he is to share his ideas about the golf swing.

10 RULES GOLFERS BREAK MOST (WITHOUT EVEN KNOWING IT)

You don't mean to step all over golf's hallowed rule book, but then you probably didn't mean to run that stop sign either. Here's *Golf for Women's* list of the rules that golfers breach with alarming regularity:

We'll be the first to admit that understanding the USGA Rules of Golf is no gimme. But at the risk of sounding like your sixth-grade homeroom teacher, we'll also remind you that golfers are expected to know and abide by them. Failing to do so increases your chances of being DQ'd at the next member-guest tournament. And if you plan to record your score for an official handicap, any rules breaches will undermine the integrity of your handicap. Here are 10 not-so-simple rules that average golfers break all the time--accidentally, of course.

1. YOU HIT A PROVISIONAL WHEN YOUR BALL MOST LIKELY LANDED IN A WATER HAZARD.

THE RULE: 27-2: If a ball may be lost outside a water hazard (including a lateral water hazard) or may be out-of-bounds, to save time a player may play another ball provisionally.

THE TRANSLATION: You cannot play a provisional ball solely because you believe the original ball might be lost in a water hazard. If you do, the second ball is not a provisional; it is in play and you incur a stroke penalty. Under the water hazard rule, you can hit from the original spot. But once you do, that ball is in play and you cannot elect to drop near the hazard. In other words, you can't re-tee and then decide what works best for you. And if you find your original ball outside of the hazard line, pick it up.
THE PENALTY: Two strokes in stroke play and loss of hole in a match.

2. YOU ASK FOR OR GIVE ADVICE.

THE RULE: 8-1: During a stipulated round, a player must not: (a) give advice to anyone in the competition playing on the

course other than [her] partner; (b) ask for advice from anyone other than [her] partner or either of their caddies.

Cont'd next page ☞

THE TRANSLATION: Golfers love to share: "How far am I?" "It looks like a 6-iron, but I'd hit a 5-iron with this wind." "Does this putt break right over the ridge?" Sound familiar? We thought so. But offering or asking for any advice that could affect the way a player executes a shot (a.k.a. "Dear Abby golf") is against the rules unless it comes from a caddie or partner. Keep your swing tips to yourself, and if you want the line on that 15-footer, pay close attention to the break of someone else's putt. (Note: The USGA has ruled that sharing general knowledge information is acceptable. For example, asking "Is the flagstick in the front or back of the green?" is okay, since the pin's location is public knowledge.)

THE PENALTY: Assess yourself two strokes for each offense and loss of hole in a match.

3. YOU IMPROVE YOUR LIE.

THE RULE: 13-1: The ball must be played as it lies.

THE TRANSLATION: Nudging the ball out of a sand-filled divot, teeing it up on a blade of grass in the rough or moving your ball away from a fence or other immovable obstruction (even if you could nick your new 7-wood) is a strict no-no.

THE PENALTY: Two strokes in stroke play and loss of hole in a match.

4. YOUR FOURSOME AGREES TO IGNORE A RULE.

THE RULE: 1-3: Players must not agree to exclude the operation of any rule or to waive any penalty incurred.

THE TRANSLATION: Your group cannot agree to take a mulligan without penalty and count your score for handicaps. That means no agreement to take breakfast balls, gimme putts or do-overs, even if your league allows it.

THE PENALTY: Disqualification of competitors concerned in stroke play and disqualification of both sides in a match.

Cont'd next page ☞

5. YOU REPLACE YOUR BALL ABOUT AN INCH IN FRONT OF THE MARKER ON THE GREEN.

THE RULE: **16-1b: A ball on the putting green may be lifted**  **and, if desired, cleaned. The position of the ball must be marked before it is lifted and the ball must be replaced.**

THE TRANSLATION: In the Rules of Golf, replaced means to place it back as closely as possible to the position the ball was in before marked. Replace does not translate to "casually move it up just a teensy-weensy bit."

THE PENALTY: **Two strokes in stroke play and loss of hole in a match.**

6. WHEN TAKING AN UNPLAYABLE LIE, YOU DROP THE BALL TWO CLUB-LENGTHS FROM THE NEAREST POINT YOU THINK IS PLAYABLE.

THE RULE: **28c: If the player deems [her] ball unplayable, [she] must, under penalty of one stroke, drop a ball within two club-lengths of the spot where the ball lay, but not nearer the hole.**

THE TRANSLATION: You take relief where the ball lies, not from the nearest point you deem playable. If you take a drop under this provision, you must measure two club-lengths from the ball's location, even if it means dropping into more trouble.

THE PENALTY: Two strokes in stroke play and loss of hole in a match.

7. YOU TAKE A PRACTICE STROKE DURING A ROUND.

THE RULE: **7-2: A player must not make a practice stroke during a round. (Note: A practice stroke is not the same as a practice swing.)**

THE TRANSLATION: No matter how badly you chili-dip a pitch shot, you cannot drop another ball for practice in an effort to improve your wedge karma (nor can you hit an old ball into the ocean or a vacant lot while you wait in the fairway). The USGA does make exceptions for practice around the green after you've holed out.

HOW TO DROP WHOM AND HOW
A ball to be dropped under the Rules must be dropped by the player himself. She must stand erect, hold the ball at shoulder height and arm's length and drop it. If a ball is dropped by any other person or in any other manner and the error is not corrected as provided in Rule 20-6, the player incurs a penalty of one stroke.

Cont'd next page ☞

THE PENALTY: Two strokes in stroke play and loss of hole in a match.

8. YOU TAKE A DROP IN THE AREA NEAR THE STAKE WHERE YOUR BALL WENT OUT-OF-BOUNDS.

THE RULE: 27-1: If a ball is lost or out-of-bounds, a player must play a ball, under penalty of one stroke, as nearly as possible to the spot from which the original ball was last played.

THE TRANSLATION: Stroke and distance. We cannot say it enough. You have to trek all the way back to play from your original spot if you are lost or out-of-bounds, even if the ball trickled out on the tail end of a 220-yard drive. So, in the interest of pace of play, always declare and hit a provisional when your ball could be lost outside a water hazard or out-of-bounds.

THE PENALTY: Two strokes in stroke play and loss of hole in a match. Note: This breach is almost always ruled "serious" by a committee and warrants disqualification if the player does not go back and play from the original spot with a penalty before she tees off on the next hole.

9. YOU TAKE EXTREME MEASURES TO IMPROVE YOUR STANCE OR LIE.

THE RULE: 13-2: A player must not improve or allow to be improved the position or lie of [her] ball, the area of [her] intended stance or swing . . . by moving, bending or breaking anything growing or fixed.

THE TRANSLATION: Leave the pruning shears at home. You can't dig up plant life or tear down branches to give yourself a clear shot. Nor may you perform circus contortions to avoid unruly vines.

THE PENALTY: Two strokes in stroke play and loss of hole in a match.

10. YOU CARRY MORE THAN 14 CLUBS.

THE RULE: 4-4: The player must start a stipulated round with not more than 14 clubs. [She] is limited to the clubs thus selected for that round except that if [she] started with fewer than 14 clubs, [she] may add any number provided her total number does not exceed 14.

THE TRANSLATION: Most players know this rule but break it unintentionally. Golfers are always adding new clubs for a round to "try them out." Remember that if you have a few extras in the bag during a round, you won't be able to submit your score to get your handicap secured before the member guest.

THE PENALTY: Two strokes for each hole you played with more than 14 clubs, with a maximum penalty of four strokes in stroke play. Deduct one hole for each hole played with more than 14 clubs, with a maximum of two holes in a match.

 Other Good Rules to Know…

HITTING AN UNATTENDED FLAGSTICK WITH A PUTT (RULE 17-3) The flagstick is in the hole, unattended, and your putt strikes it. That's a 2-stroke penalty in stroke play (ball subsequently played as it lies) and loss of hole in match play.

Cont'd next page ☞

A CLEAN GREEN

WHAT AM I ALLOWED TO USE TO CLEAN OFF DEBRIS ON THE GREEN? The restriction on how loose impediments (natural objects, such as stones, leaves and twigs) may be removed from a line of putt was revised in the 2004 edition of the Rules of Golf (see Rule 16-1a). You can now touch your line with your hand, club, towel, cap, ham sandwich—you name it—in order to remove loose impediments.

WHAT IS THE MAXIMUM NUMBER OF STROKES THAT A PERSON MUST COUNT ON HOLES—PAR 3, PAR 4 OR PAR 5?
Your score for the hole is the total number of strokes it takes to get the ball in the hole, plus all penalty strokes. However, after

the round you need to adjust your score for handicap-posting purposes only (see Section 4-3 of the USGA Handicap System Manual). This means that you are only allowed to count a certain maximum number of strokes.

GROUNDING THE CLUB IN A HAZARD (RULE 13-4)
Grounding the club in a hazard is illegal. Anyone who does it must assess themselves (or have assessed) a 2-stroke penalty (or loss of hole in match play).

BALL MOVES AFTER ADDRESS (RULE 18-2B)
If your ball moves once you've taken your address, it's a 1-stroke penalty. The ball is replaced on its original spot.

YES

DO NOT GROUND YOUR CLUB IN A HAZARD

Ball Moves after Loose Impediment is Removed (Rule 18-2c)
Players can remove loose impediments without penalty as long as the ball and the loose impediment are not both in a hazard. Through the green, if the ball moves when any loose impediment within one club length of the ball is removed, it's a 1-stroke penalty. The ball is replaced at the original spot.

KNOW YOUR
ETIQUETTE

A Girl's On-Course **Survival Guide** to Golf™

Golf is a game that could ruffle Emily Post. But committing breaches in etiquette can brand you as a lightweight and are embarrassing to boot. Here's a quick primer on how you should always—and never—behave, from first swing to final handshake.

1. NEVER miss your tee time. Running late won't endear you to your playing partners, so set your alarm clock. If you're playing a new course, get directions beforehand. To avoid fruitless searches around an unfamiliar club, pick a time and place to meet your host.

2. ALWAYS introduce yourself when playing as a guest. People who work at private clubs know their members, and therefore they'll know you're not one of them. You'll save yourself awkward conversations with pro shop staff, locker-room attendants and others by telling them whose guest you are right off the bat.

3. ALWAYS know the agenda. Nothing is worse than finding out there's a lunch or dinner planned, and the rest of the group has changed into cocktail-party attire while you're stuck in your grubby golf clothes.

Cont'd next page ☞

4. NEVER go in clueless. Ask the host in advance with whom you'll be playing. This will help you get a read on the level of play.

5. ALWAYS find out what the cart rules are before the round. Practicing the 90-degree rule on a path-only day can ensure that your first invitation will be your last.

6. ALWAYS have a handicap. Playing in member/guest, charity, and club events without one is poor etiquette. And bring your card.

7. NEVER treat your caddie like a Sherpa. Lighten his-or-her load. Remove the extra dozen or so balls you've stashed in your bag and your raingear if you don't need it, plus any other excess equipment. Hernia operations are expensive.

8. NEVER cell out. Gabbing on your cell phone during a round, especially if you're a guest at a club, is the height of rudeness. First, find out if the club allows cell phones at all. If you must use your phone (baby-sitter alert!), use it sparingly. Ideally, you should turn it off before a round (or set it to vibrate), put it in

GABBING ON YOUR CELL PHONE DURING A
ROUND IS THE HEIGHT OF RUDENESS. NOT TO
MENTION DRIVING PAST A PLAYER WHILE
SHE IS ADDRESSING THE BALL!!

your bag, and check it once at the turn. When possible, call from
the clubhouse or locker room, and keep it brief.

9. ALWAYS take one practice swing. Not three, not five, not nine. One.

Cont'd next page

10. NEVER tee off in front of the markers. It's a double no-no because technically it violates the rules (the penalty is two shots in stroke play).

11. ALWAYS hit a provisional ball if you think there's a chance that your ball is lost outside of a water hazard or out of bounds.

12. NEVER crowd the player who's hitting or putting. Stand at least two club lengths behind and one club length to either side.

13. NEVER move a loose impediment in a bunker. Not a leaf, not a rock, not a speck of pollen. Doing so is a rules violation, and besides, your partners will notice.

14. NEVER dawdle at the tee or anywhere else. Slow play is one of the greatest breaches of etiquette, and if you're not ready to hit, you're contributing to it. Know your yardage, have your club selected, and be prepared to play.

15. Tip the valet: $1 when he takes your car; $1 when he returns it safely.

16. Tip the locker-room attendant: $1 for a towel; $2 if she cleans your shoes.

17. Tip the caddie: $15 per bag; $20 to $25 if he or she saved you strokes.

18. Tip the forecaddie: $10; $15 if he scaled mountains to track down your errant shots.

NEVER MOVE A LOOSE IMPEDIMENT IN THE BUNKER. NOT A LEAF, NOT A ROCK, NOT A SPECK OF POLLEN. AND DEFINITELY NOT A TURTLE.

Cont'd next page ☞

19. Tip the club cleaner: $3; $5 if you took up a ton of turf during the round.

20. ALWAYS give a heads-up on cell calls. Let your group know if you anticipate having to make a call. If you do and it lasts longer than expected, take yourself out of the hole.

21. NEVER walk in another player's line. This is the golden rule of etiquette. But also make sure to avoid the through line, which is the same line past the hole that the ball would take if the player misses it long. Only a true golf nut or Michelle Wie would know what you're talking about.

22. ALWAYS stop the cart when players are hitting. Be conscious not only of your group but also groups playing neighboring holes. And look twice before you throw the cart into reverse; that high-pitched noise can give someone the shanks.

23. NEVER drink too much and drive. This includes overindulging on the course and on the way home. Keep it light or save the cocktails for after the round. If you overdo it, relinquish your car keys.

24. ALWAYS buy your caddie a (nonalcoholic) beverage at the turn. It's the least you can do after he or she has chased your ball for nine holes. The better you treat caddies, the more likely they are to save you strokes.

25. ALWAYS ask politely to play through. The most convenient time is right after the group ahead has teed off on the next hole and you're waiting behind them. If you are holding up play, offer to let the group behind you play through. Usually, a par-3 is the easiest place to do so.

26. NEVER enter fairway and greenside bunkers from the high side. Climbing down steep inclines can damage the bunker, so go in low.

NEVER WALK IN ANOTHER PLAYER'S LINE.
THIS IS THE GOLDEN RULE OF ETIQUETTE.

27. NEVER drive your cart near a green or a bunker. Course superintendents and greenkeepers everywhere will curse you for this offense, and deservedly so.

Cont'd next page ☞

28. ALWAYS ask before tending the flag. The player whose ball is closest to the hole should tend. As long as a player has a putter in her hand, even if she's off the green, you should ask if she wants the flag tended. And like Peter Pan, be mindful of your shadow; it shouldn't cross the hole or the line.

29. ALWAYS make like a librarian and be quiet when your playing partners are hitting or putting. No whispers, zippers, Velcro sounds, or club clanking, please.

30. ALWAYS fix your pitch marks—with a proper repair tool, please. Tees are for the tee box, not for ball marking or green repair.

31. NEVER ground your club in a hazard or a bunker. Not only is it a rules infraction, it's an etiquette breach as well: Knowing the basic rules is part of the game.

YES

32. ALWAYS mark your ball properly on the green. The best way is to place the marker behind the ball without touching it.

33. NEVER touch a ball to identify it. Mark your ball clearly with a Sharpie before the round and memorize the brand and number before you play it.

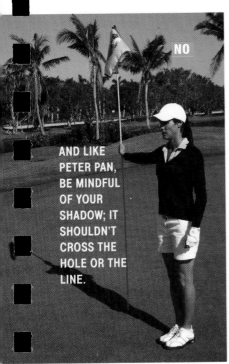

NO

AND LIKE PETER PAN, BE MINDFUL OF YOUR SHADOW; IT SHOULDN'T CROSS THE HOLE OR THE LINE.

34. ALWAYS drop the ball properly when you're taking relief. Stand facing the hole with your arm out at shoulder height and drop the ball.

35. NEVER cop an attitude. Profanity will not improve your score— besides, it's tacky and unladylike—neither will huffing and puffing after each shot.

36. ALWAYS be gracious. Everyone appreciates a good sport. On the flip side,

Cont'd next page ☞

if your playing partners are struggling and you're on your game, try to keep the Sergio Garcia antics to a minimum. No one appreciates a show-off.

37. NEVER place your bag on the green or the fringe. The bag stand and the weight can damage the green. Place it away from the putting surface and on the way to the next tee to speed up play.

38. ALWAYS know the club policies. Call ahead to find out the dress code and the cell phone policy and whether or not cash is used on the premises.

39. ALWAYS repair your divots. Failing to take care of the course will reflect badly on you and your host. If you are playing on Bermuda grass, fill the divot with sand. If you are playing on bent grass, replace the divots exactly as you dug them up.

40. NEVER drop or slam the flagstick against the green. The surface can easily dent. After you've pulled the pin, gently place it on or near the fringe, away from anyone's view or line.

41. ALWAYS pick up when you're playing a match and you're out of a hole. The pros do it when they're playing casually to speed up play; you should, too.

42. ALWAYS mind your clubs. If you forget one and remember it within two holes, go back, but hit your shot first. Approach the group behind you carefully and ask if they have found a club. If you can't recall where you left

NO · **YES**

ALWAYS KNOW THE CLUB POLICIES. CALL
AHEAD TO FIND OUT THE DRESS CODE.

the club, wait until the round is over, go to the pro
shop and ask if anyone has turned in your club. If
not, leave your name and number.

43. NEVER leave a round without returning the host's
invitation. Even if you're not a member of a club
yourself, invite your friend to join you at a public
course or for lunch in the near future.

Cont'd next page ☞

44. **ALWAYS** pay up. If you've made a wager on a round and you lose, fork over what you owe.

45. **ALWAYS** have fun. Isn't that the point?

46. **ALWAYS** express your appreciation. Following a round, shake hands with your partners and thank them for the game.

47. **WHO SHOULD DRIVE THE CART IN A MIXED GROUP?**
The man doesn't automatically drive. The host player drives the cart; he or she knows the layout and service areas on the course. It helps to move play along.

48. **HOW DO I AVOID EMBARRASSMENT WHEN MEN CLIENTS INSIST ON PAYING?** Your client is your guest during the time that you spend on the course. If you pay in advance by credit card, you can avoid the hassle of who pays.

49. **WHAT ABOUT SHOES?**
When playing at a corporate outing or a private club, never change them in the parking lot. We call this person a "trunk slammer." Invest in a shoe bag and use the locker room to change your shoes. If you can't, make the switch in your car.

50. **WHEN IS THE BEST TIME TO DISCUSS BUSINESS?**
Use your time wisely; don't rush it. During the early holes, learn about your client's interests. If business doesn't come up naturally, stay on generalities until the 19th hole, when you can talk turkey.

51. HOW DO I DEAL WITH A MACHO MEMBER OF A GROUP? Let him beat his chest; he only hurts himself. Know when to listen and when to tune him out. And by all means, win.

DIVOT REPAIR MIX

ALWAYS REPAIR YOUR DIVOTS. IF YOU ARE PLAYING ON BERMUDA GRASS, FILL THE DIVOT WITH SAND. IF YOU ARE PLAYING ON BENT GRASS, REPLACE THE DIVOTS EXACTLY AS YOU DUG THEM UP.

WHAT THE HECK IS A SQUARE??!!

Golf has its own language which includes some pretty strange-sounding words. Here is a quick reference of the most common golf terms and phrases that every golfer should know.

ACE, aka *hole-in-one* A hole finished in one stroke, typically on par 3's.

ADDRESS Position taken by a player prior to hitting a shot. According to the Rules of Golf, a player has "addressed" the ball when she has taken her stance and grounded her club. Commonly referred to as "addressing the ball."

APPROACH SHOT A shot played to the putting surface.

AWAY The ball that is the greatest distance from the hole when more than one golfer is playing. It is the first ball to be played.

BACKSPIN A reverse spin placed on the ball. Achieved when a player compresses the ball, which refers to hitting down on the back of the ball.

BALL EMBEDDED, aka *plugged* a ball stuck in the ground as a result of its impact. Example: As part of the Rules of Golf you are permitted to lift, clean, and then drop an embedded ball without penalty.

BALL IN PLAY A ball is in play as soon as the player has made a stroke in the tee-off area. It remains in play until it is holed out, except when it is out of bounds, lost, lifted, or when another ball is substituted in accordance with the rules.

BALL MARKER A token or a small coin used to spot the ball's position on the green prior to lifting it.

BIRDIE One stroke under par for a hole. Example: score of 2 on a par 3.

BLOCK A shot that veers off-line, typically right, as the result of an open clubface through impact.

BOGEY A score of 1 over par for the hole. Example: score of 5 on a par 4.

BREAK The way in which the ball will roll or bounce.

BURIED LIE A ball partially buried beneath the sand in a bunker.

CASUAL WATER Any temporary accumulations of water that is not a hazard or in a water hazard. A player may lift her ball from casual water without penalty.

CHIP SHOT A shot typically played from very close to the green, usually within a few yards of the putting surface.

CHUNKEY MONKEY, aka *Chunk Shot, Chili Dip or Fat* When the club hits the ground behind the ball, resulting in a missed shot.

Cont'd next page ☞

CLOSED STANCE **A stance in which body lines (shoulders, hips and feet) are positioned right of the intended target line.**

COCK, aka *wrist hinge* **To bend the wrists backwards in the backswing.**

COLLAR **The grassy fringe surrounding the putting green.**

CUT SHOT, aka *fade* **A controlled shot that results in a left-to-right ball flight.**

DIVOT **A piece of turf removed by the club when making a shot. It is always replaced or filled with divot mix.**

DOGLEG **A left or right bend in the fairway.**

DOUBLE BOGEY **A score of 2 over par for a single hole. Example: score of 7 on a par 5.**

DRAW SHOT **A shot that produces a right-to-left ball flight.**

DROP **To deposit the ball on the course, dropped at shoulder height and at arms length, in order to put the ball back into play after it has been declared unplayable, lost, or in a hazard.**

EAGLE **Two strokes under par for a single hole. Example: score of 3 on a par 5.**

CLUBFACE **The hitting area or surface of the clubhead.**

FADE, aka *cut* **A shot that produces a left-to-right ball flight.**

FAIRWAY The well-maintained area of the course between the tee and the green, that allows a good lie for the ball.

FAT SHOT The club hits the ground behind the ball, resulting in high or low shots with a loss of distance.

FLIER LIE A ball is hit without spin and goes a greater distance than normal. Typically occurs out of the rough.

FOLLOW-THROUGH The continuation of the swing after the ball has been hit.

FRIED-EGG A ball half-buried in the sand.

FRINGE The area surrounding the putting green, sometimes cut to a height lower than the fairway but not as short as the green itself.

GRAIN The direction the grass on the green is growing.

GREENS IN REGULATION To achieve a green in regulation, your ball must be on the putting surface in the expected number of strokes in relation to par. Example: for a par 5, your ball must be on the putting surface in 3 strokes.

GREENSIDE BUNKER Adjacent to the putting green.

GROUNDING THE CLUB Placing the clubhead behind the ball at address. Grounding the club is not allowed in a hazard.

Cont'd next page ☞

GROUND UNDER REPAIR Any part of the course being repaired is ground under repair. A ball that lands in such an area must be removed without penalty.

HAZARD Any sand trap, bunker, or water on the course.

HOOK A shot that produces a sharp right-to-left ball flight.

HOSEL The hollow part of an iron clubhead into which the shaft is fitted.

IMPACT The moment the ball strikes the club.

INTENDED LINE The line you expect the ball to travel after it is hit.

LAG To putt the ball with the intention of leaving it short, to ensure being able to hole out on the next stroke.

LATERAL HAZARD Any hazard running parallel to the line of play.

LAY UP To play a shorter shot than might normally be attempted. Would be done to achieve a good lie short of a hazard rather than trying to hit the green in one less shot.

LIE The position in which the ball rests on the ground.

LIP The top rim of the hole or cup, where the sand meets the edge of the grass in a bunker.

LOFT A measurement, in degrees, of the angle at which the face of the club lies relative to a perfectly vertical face. The higher the loft, the higher the ball flight.

LOOSE IMPEDIMENTS Any natural object that is not fixed or growing. This can include loose stones, twigs, branches, or turtles.

MATCH PLAY A competition played with each hole being a separate game. A player winning the most holes, rather than having the lowest score, is the winner. For example, the winner of the first hole is "one up." Even if the player wins that hole by two or three strokes, she is still only "one up." The lead is increased every time the player wins another hole. The winner is the one who wins the most holes. This was the original form of golf competition.

MULLIGAN A second shot that is allowed on the first tee to be taken in friendly play when the player has missed the first one. Not allowed by the Rules of Golf.

LIFT-CLEAN-AND-PLACE A rule that allows a player to mark her ball, so that she can clean the ball and place it back no greater than 6 inches from original spot or no closer to the hole.

OBSTRUCTION Any artificial object that has been left or placed on the course, with the exception of course boundary markers and constructed roads and paths.

OPEN FACE refers to the position of the clubface relative to the target line at impact (the moment the clubface strikes the ball). Will result in a ball that starts well right of the target line.

OPEN STANCE A stance in which body lines (shoulders, hips and feet) are positioned left of the target line.

Cont'd next page ☞

OUT OF BOUNDS The area outside of the course in which play is prohibited, typically indicated by white stakes. A player is penalized stroke and distance for going out of bounds. That is, she must replay the shot with a penalty of one stroke.

PAR The number of strokes a player should take to complete a round with good performance. Par for each hole is given on the scorecard.

PENALTY STROKE An additional stroke added to a player's score for a rules violation.

PICK-UP To pickup one's ball before holing out. In match play, this concedes the hole, in stroke play, incurs disqualification.

PIN PLACEMENT (PIN POSITION) The position of a hole on a putting green on any given day.

PLANE A term used to describe the path (angle) of the club shaft relative to your body during the swing.

PLAYING THROUGH Passing another group of players who are playing ahead, typically because they are playing too slowly.

POP-UP A short, high shot typically the result of a ball teed up to high or of incorrect swing mechanics.

PREFERRED LIE Local rules which allow a player to improve her lie in a specific manner without penalty. For example, if the lift-clean-and-place rule is in effect due to heavy rains or snow.

PROVISIONAL BALL A ball played if the previously played ball was lost or out of bounds.

PULL A ball that veers to the left of the intended target line, typically the result of incorrect swing mechanics.

PUNCH SHOT Low, controlled shot typically used to get under a tree or obstruction or to keep the ball flight low.

PUSH A ball that veers to the right of the intended target line, typically the result of incorrect swing mechanics. Opposite of PULL.

READING THE GREEN Determining the path that the ball will take on its way to the hole by analyzing the contour and texture (grain) of the green.

RELEASE The point in the downswing where you uncock your wrists.

ROUGH Long grass areas adjacent to fairway, greens, tees or hazards.

SAND TRAP The common name for a bunker.

SANDY Making par after being in a bunker. Example: one shot out of the bunker and a one-putt.

SCRATCH GOLFER A player who has a handicap of 0. This player will theoretically shoot even par or better every time out. Christina's goal this millennium.

Cont'd next page ☞

SCOOP An improper swing in which the club has a digging or scooping action, typically the result of improper wrist action through impact.

SET UP To position yourself for the address.

SHANK A shot struck by the club's hosel. Typically travels violently to the right of the intended target line.

SHORT GAME The part of the game that is made up of chip shots, pitching, and putting.

SHORT IRONS The highly lofted irons such as a sand wedge, pitching wedge, 9-iron, and 8-iron.

SIDEHILL LIE A lie with the ball either above or below your feet.

SKULLING Hitting the ball at or above its center, causing the ball to be hit too hard and travel too great a distance.

SLICE A shot that curves strongly from left to right as a result of sidespin, typically the result of flaws in swing mechanics.

SNAP-HOOK To hit a shot with an acute, low, right-to-left ball flight.

SQUARE STANCE When your clubface is perpendicular to the target line and your feet, hips, and shoulders are all parallel to the target line.

SQUARE AT IMPACT or **SQUARE FACE** refers to the position of the clubface relative to the target line at impact. A square face is one in which the club is neither open or closed, an ideal position at impact.

STANCE The position of your feet when addressing the ball.

STROKE The forward motion of the clubhead made with the intent to hit the ball whether contact is made or not.

TAKE-AWAY The start of the backswing.

TEXAS BUGRUNNER or **WORMBURNER** A ball hit with adequate distance and that hugs the ground.

THIN The ball is above center with the clubhead, typically resulting in a low-to-the-ground shot.

TOE The part of the clubhead farthest from where it joins the shaft.

TOP THE BALL To hit the ball above its center, causing it to roll or hop rather than get airborne.

TRIPLE BOGEY, aka *SNOWMAN* This term is used when a golfer is 3 over par on a hole. Example: score of 7 on a par 4.

UP-AND-DOWN Getting in the hole from off the green in 2 shots. Example: one shot on the green and a one-putt into the hole.

WAGGLE Movement of the clubhead prior to swinging.

WHIFF To swing and miss the ball, typically an embarrassing moment.

YIPS Shakiness or nervousness in making a shot.